STORIES AND SONGS

BORN IN THE COUNTY

by

4/21/96

ROGER W. TAYLOR

To Candy,
Hope you like
the Stories +
Songs.

Roger W Taylor

Kestrel Productions
Ballwin, Missouri

© 1995 Roger W. Taylor
Kestrel Productions
674 Meramec Dr.
Ballwin, Missouri 63021-7232

ISBN 0-9649726-0-3

DEDICATION

To my grandchildren —
Jacob, Andrew, Michael and Zachary.

and

To Martin the guitar, who was once pronounced dead, but after having been resurrected from a trash bin, was patched up and performed beautifully in the musical portion of this work. His participation gives added meaning to the song "The West County Dump."

and

To the Wildwood Spirit. While we can debate the pros and cons of the Wildwood incorporation, I applaud its vision and the tenacity of the folks who finally said, "Enough is enough, we'll take care of our own stuff, thank you." How refreshing!

ACKNOWLEDGMENTS

This work never would have reached completion if it hadn't been for a large number of supportive individuals who gave willingly of their time and moral support. It would be impossible to name them all, but I would like to at least thank the following individuals, institutions, and government agencies.

At the top of the list in producing the music portion of *STORIES AND SONGS* is Roger Guth, who in addition to playing drums, piano, and keyboard, shared in the vocals and also produced and arranged the work. Jim Mayer not only played bass but did the mixing and recording. Rick Haydon played the guitars, Sandy Weltman the harmonica and juice harp. I also want to thank Betty and Roger Oliver for their Studio 88 hospitality, and Keith Pinkston of Shadow and Razor Boy records for having the cover designed and the tapes and CD's produced.

For the story portion of this work, I want to thank the following:

In tracing the Franke family background, LaVerne and Cindy Guth helped piece together much of the family's genealogical history and also provided many of the family's photos. Others who were also extremely helpful in this area were Mildred Struessel, as were Vernon and Bill Franke. It was interesting how difficult it was to get basic information about the Franke family. Apparently the old folks talked little about those early years and the "Old Country." It's my impression that they were a very mellow yet stoic and pragmatic people who arrived here with the barest of cultural necessities — just the basics. Once unpacked, they adapted to their new surroundings, worked hard, set down new roots, and never looked back.

As for the Taylor side of the family, I want to thank my late Grandfather Taylor and Aunt Helen Vantuyl for their storytelling abilities. Anita Taylor was also helpful in clearing up some of the facts related to my Uncle Warren's transition from dairy farmer to excavator.

I also want to thank those individuals who provided information on environmental issues and reviewed those sections: Kay Drey, one of our country's leading anti-nuclear activists, who reviewed the section on nuclear waste disposal; Stephen H. McCracken, manager of the Weldon Spring Site; my son Steven Taylor, who kept me abreast of the status of the Times Beach dioxin incinerator and reviewed that section of the book; Stephanie Lickerman, who provided information and reviewed the section on efforts to establish a county Tree Ordinance as well as the Wildwood controversy.

Councilman Greg Quinn of the Seventh District and his Administrative Assistant George Heil were most helpful in locating source materials pertaining to the County Government, as were June Fowler and Joe Bujnich of the Department of Planning and Esley Hamilton of the Department of Parks and Recreation. Joe Trinko and Steven Parker from the State Department of Natural Resources Regional Office and William R. Iseminger of Cahokia Mounds State Historic Site also gave freely of their time. Others who provided assistance were Rich Love, Superintendent of Castlewood State Park, and Sharon Farris, President of the Castlewood Association.

A large number of resource materials were used throughout. I relied heavily on local newspapers to chart past and current issues. In particular, I found the St. Louis Post-Dispatch February 1989 series titled "St. Louis' Nuclear Waste" very helpful, as I did their December 12, 1982, feature article titled "Toxic Trail Through Missouri," which provided historic background on how dioxin was spread throughout the state. Two books on the history of St. Louis were particularly helpful — Ernest Kirschten's *Catfish and Crystal,* New York 1960 and James Neal Primm's *Lion of the Valley: St. Louis Missouri,* Boulder, Colorado, 1981 which is still in print. The Mercantile Library and the St. Louis office for the Missouri Coalition of the Environment were also very helpful.

Thanks also to Glen Weathers who helped to reproduce many of the family photos, Denise Eitzen Gibson who laid out the book for printing, and in particular Sara Jenkins who was helpful in so many ways.

Also I would like to thank my son Ken Taylor, Joan Frazier and Judy Furman who over the last few years gently pushed me into the computer age. Last but not least, my wife Jenny provided me with all the space I needed to work on the project and at the same time helped to keep me on task. To all the above and many more, thanks again!

PREFACE

STORIES AND SONGS is the product of a long evolutionary process. Some 30 or more years ago, just for the fun of it, I started composing songs on my way to and from many of my lone canoe trips and daily drives to and from work. By 1982 I had quite a collection of songs, most of which dealt with Missouri rivers as well as local and national environmental issues. After I wrote down some of the songs, I realized that each one told a story, and collectively they formed a bigger story. Placed in chronological order, these stories and songs present a summary of the human and environmental history of the area, particularly from the post-World War II period to the present.

In 1993, after 30 years in the eighth grade, I finally graduated and retired from teaching. I had incorporated many of the songs into my classroom lessons and public presentations and now wanted to put them to music and have them recorded. Not having any musical training, I needed someone who had experience in such matters and would be interested in such a project. That person turned out to be my second cousin on my mother's side of the family, Roger Guth.

Roger grew up helping his parents work one of the few remaining truck farms in South St. Louis County. From both of his parents he inherited a love for the land as well as for music. By the time he graduated from high school, he had become an accomplished musician. Eventually he teamed up with the Mayer brothers, Jim and Peter, to form the group PM, which developed a large local following. Word of their writing and performing skills soon began to spread. They eventually signed a contract with Warner Brothers, produced an album, and began working with a number of top recording artists. For the last eight years the group has served as the core of Jimmy Buffett's rhythm section and have collaborated with him on a number of songs and albums. They also continue to record and perform on their own. Thus, I was more than pleased when Roger agreed to take time from his busy schedule to be the musical director and arranger for this material.

Born in the County is the first of what we hope will be a series of *STORIES AND SONGS*. This project is in no way meant to be a complete work, but a sweeping overview of human interaction and impact upon the St. Louis area—St. Louis County in particular. This companion book provides a more extensive historical background for the songs on the recordings.

Part One, From Wilderness To Statehood, takes a brief look at the impact of human activity on the environment of the St. Louis area from the time of the first Americans — the original inhabitants of the continent — to Missouri's statehood.

Part Two, Rooted, begins with the story of life in the Gravois Creek area of South St. Louis County just prior to the Civil War when my great-grandfather Carl Franke settled there. It continues with the arrival of my grandfather Roy Richie Taylor and his family during the Great Depression and concludes with the period I grew up in, when the area was being transformed from a predominately rural to a suburban area.

Part Three, Beyond the Brier Patch, covers the time period from the early 1960's until I moved to Village of Castlewood in 1978 and takes a brief look at the early environmental history of our country and the state of Missouri as well as some of the major environmental issues that affected the St. Louis area in particular.

Part Four, Reality Check, deals with some of our current community/ environmental problems, especially urban development and how it impacts on the natural and human community.

Part Five, The Quest, is a short transitional piece that was written after I completed the main text and did the update on the current issues covered in Part Four. It reflects upon our changing relationship with our natural environment as well as our sense of community.

Part Six, Update, brings current issues up to date and ends with my personal observations.

At the end of the text is a timeline that includes major events and other interesting tidbits of information related to our history.

My focus throughout this work is our relationship to the land and the environment and our ever-changing sense of community. I hope that after reading the words and listening to the music, the reader's perception of time and place will be deeper and more finely tuned.

As the reader will soon find out, I consider myself what is today referred to as an "environmentalist." Many of you will disagree with me on various issues. That's fine. As I've always told my students, "This is America, and you have the right to disagree with me, even though I'm right!"

A few sections of this text parallel portions of my previous books, *Watershed–1* and *Watershed–2*, which deal with the history of the first white (Euro-American) settlement in the state of Missouri.

I hope you enjoy this first volume of *STORIES AND SONGS* as much as Roger Guth and I enjoyed putting it together.

Roger W. Taylor
Nuthatch
Castlewood, Missouri
October 21, 1995

CONTENTS

Songs are indicated in italic. Those in bold italic are on the CD and tape.

PICTURES – PHOTOS – MAPS

Cahokia, Illinois, 900–1300 A.D.
The center of Mississippian culture was located on land included in the
present-day St. Louis metropolitan area.
Painting by William R. Iseminger,
courtesy of Cahokia Mounds State Historic Site.

PART I

FROM WILDERNESS TO STATEHOOD

"We have not inherited the land from our fathers, we are borrowing it from our children."

—The First Americans

    Much has been written about biological heredity, cultural heritage, and social interactions, much less about the importance of our interactions with our natural environment. To some of us, the latter could be considered the most important single factor in the development of our being. I feel that this is true in my case, and even more so for those who preceded me: the First Americans, the French, the Spanish, the American frontiersmen, and the German immigrants who were my ancestors. So, let me begin my story by telling you about the natural environment and those who preceded me to a place, the area known today as St. Louis, Missouri.

    From the time of its origins in 1763 until the "great split" in 1876, St. Louis City and County were a single entity. Even today there is much cultural, political, and geographical overlapping. So, for practical reasons, the city and the county as well as neighboring communities on both sides of the Mississippi River are often viewed here as a single entity — what we refer to as the St. Louis Metropolitan Area. This area includes the cities of St. Louis, on both sides of the river, and the counties of St. Louis, St. Charles, Jefferson, Franklin, Warren, and Lincoln in Missouri, and Monroe, St. Clair, Clinton, Madison, and Jersey in Illinois.

1

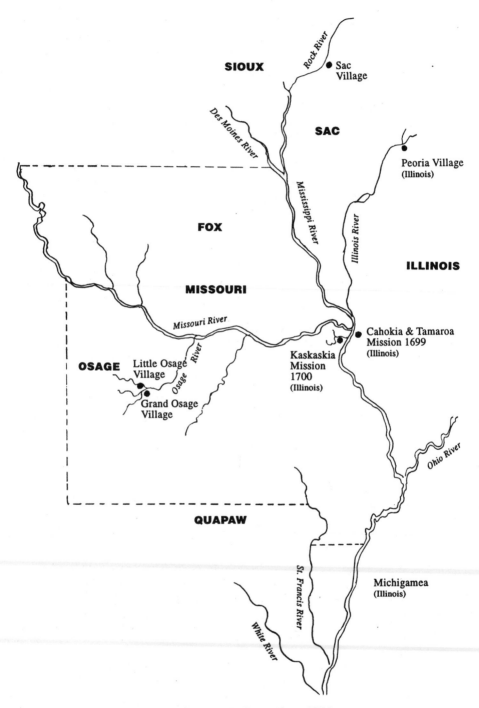

SIOUX

Rock River

● Sac
Village

Des Moines River

SAC

Peoria Village
(Illinois)

Mississippi River

Illinois River

FOX

MISSOURI

ILLINOIS

Missouri River

Cahokia & Tamaroa
Mission 1699
(Illinois)

OSAGE   Little Osage
Village

Osage River

Kaskaskia
Mission
1700
(Illinois)

Grand Osage
Village

Ohio River

QUAPAW

St. Francis River

Michigamea
(Illinois)

White River

Map showing Indian tribes, 1700.

1 - Before Laclede: The First Americans

It's no accident that St. Louis is located at the confluence of the nation's two greatest rivers, the Missouri and the Mississippi. They merge here like two huge arteries, and along with the Illinois, the Ohio, and smaller vessels and capillaries, they function as the heart of our nation's circulatory system, pumping their life-giving fluids through most of the country. The Mississippi watershed extends east to the western slope of the Appalachians and west to the eastern slope of the Rockies. It empties its waters into the Gulf of Mexico after having nourished thirty-two American states and two Canadian provinces. It extends eastward to within 250 miles of the Atlantic and westward to within 500 miles of the Pacific.

The watershed provided fertile plains that produced lush vegetation, which over the millenniums drew both wildlife and the first Americans. The river and its tributaries also serve as one of the world's largest natural highway systems. Thus, it should come as no surprise that the St. Louis area once served as the center of the great mound-building Mississippian culture. At its height, just prior to the arrival of Europeans, there was an estimated population of 20-30,000 — the largest concentration of humans in the Americas north of Mexico. Satellite communities were found up and down the watershed reaching as far south as the Ohio River and as far west on the Missouri as the Kansas City area.

The Mississippians actually lived on both sides of the river, but because of its highly fertile floodplain, the center of their culture was at present-day Cahokia, Illinois. These people were not only the most agri-cultural Indians north of Mexico, but also were skilled artisans and the region's most active traders. They bartered their wares along the inland waterways, traveling north to Lake Superior where they acquired copper; south to the Gulf for shells, alligator teeth, and shark skin; up the Ohio for mica; and westward on the Missouri for obsidian and the teeth of the grizzly bear.

The Mississippians flourished between 900–1300 AD, then suddenly vanished. What caused the demise of this once great culture has been a matter of speculation. Archaeological records show that, like the Indians to the south, they had become increasingly dependent on maize (corn). Along with increasing food surpluses came the accumulation of wealth and increased division of labor. The historical record throughout the world shows that when that happens, a struggle for wealth and power soon follows.

3

In addition to the possibility of inter-social strife, some historians theorize that, as was the case in the Roman Empire and among the Pueblo Indians of our Southwest, food surpluses as well as other material wealth proved tempting to the Mississippians' neighboring tribes. The fact that Cahokia was surrounded by a fourteen-foot wooden stockade suggests that from time to time it was subjected to siege.

We know that the Mississippian dependence on maize as their main food staple paralleled a reduction of their artistic output as well as increased health risks such as the loss of bone density. Some also believe the large concentration of people led to critical fuel shortages and the reduction in numbers of large game species. Whatever the reason, by the time the Europeans arrived, all that remained on the east and west sides of the river were the Indian mounds.

Following the collapse of the Mississippians and up until the arrival of the Europeans, the area served as home to a tribe of Sioux who lived near the mouth of the river that now bears their name. There were also several tribes of the Illinois Nation: the Tamaroa, Cahokia, Michigamea, and Kaskaskia, who were of Algonquin stock. The Illinois, like the Sioux of the plains, once lived to the north around the Great Lakes.

The Osage, a branch of the Sioux and the tribe we most associate with the state of Missouri, were primarily prairie not river people, and their main settlements were from Central Missouri westward into Kansas. Before the arrival of the Europeans, they primarily visited our area on a seasonal basis.

Just prior to the arrival of the Europeans, most of the Illinois were living along the Mississippi and tributaries from what are today the states of Illinois, Iowa, and Missouri southward into Arkansas. In fact, it was Father Marquette's Jesuit Mission of the Immaculate Conception among the Kaskaskia Indians that settled for several seasons at the mouth of the River Des Peres which today serves as the southern boundary of St. Louis City. That first Euro-American settlement in the state of Missouri was in 1700, long before the creation of Ste. Genevieve around 1750, St. Louis in 1762, and Carondelet 1767.

The Indians of the area lived in tribal villages. Their homes were not teepees like the highly nomadic plains Indians but long houses. These were semi-permanent homes built of arched saplings and covered with bark or grass. Individual residences often housed extended families including a husband with one or more wives, their children, and often their daughter's family.

Among the Illinois each family had its own individual fireplace in their communal lodges, thus individual lodges had many fireplaces. French officials kept records of the size of each village by the number of fireplaces they could count.

4

As was the case of the Kaskaskia at River Des Peres, tribal units clustered together along the rivers and streams. The waterways were traveled in dugout canoes called pirogues. The village women planted communal food plots of maize, squash, beans, and pumpkin. Men hunted and fished the immediate area. After the maize crop sprouted and was "hilled", they went off on the first seasonal hunt across the Great River to the "East Side" where they hunted buffalo. They returned to their home base in time to harvest their crops, spend the rest of the summer, and prepare for their fall-winter hunt.

Following harvest, they once again crossed the river where they constructed smaller temporary villages. There they gathered furs and dried enough buffalo meat to take them through the winter. It was during these winter hunts that the men often broke up into small raiding parties to attack their enemies, the Sac, the Fox, and Sioux to the north, the Cherokee and their allies to the south, and the Osage to the west. In like manner, they experienced counterattacks. Such intertribal warfare over thousands of seasons had been well integrated into their culture and was part of each young man's rite of passage. Not only was he required to prove himself as a hunter but also as a warrior before he would be accepted by the other men and before he could consider marriage. In the early spring, they returned to their homes, and the cycle was repeated once again.

Being hunters, gathers, and warriors, other than burning the prairie from time to time to keep the hardwoods at bay, the local Indians had little impact on their environment. They were master adapters, and prior to the arrival of the Europeans, they had little economic motivation to do otherwise.

Life for the local Indians was seasonal and largely predictable. They could roll with most any ecological punch Ma Nature might throw at them. If the rivers or small streams such as the Des Peres flooded their villages, or their crops failed, the loss was not a catastrophe, as is often the case today. For these highly successful omnivores, relocation or alteration in diet would be a minor inconvenience. There were no Red Cross units, no Salvation Army, no food stamps, no Division of Human Resources. They were group-sufficient. When they moved, they didn't have to rent a U-Haul; what they couldn't carry or load in canoes didn't go. What was left behind was biodegradable and easily recycled back into the natural system. Their way of life involved no complex and costly collection systems, no debate over incinerators, no hazardous waste sites. They left the rivers and streams as pristine as when they first arrived.

Young and old alike had a strong sense of their place in the community as well as their universe, and the tribal unit lived as a tight, interdependent community. That unit took its nourishment, its living, directly from the land. Thus, the land and the rivers were their constant

5

provider. Under such a system, few tribal laws were required. Government was pure and simple: "Thou shall live within the laws of nature, or perish."

Because of their sparse populations, modern-day problems such as overcrowding, famine, and contagious disease were strangers to their camps. An estimated one million Americans were living in North America north of Mexico before the arrival of the Europeans. Just think about it — two and a half times more people live in the St. Louis Metropolitan Area today than lived in all of North America before the arrival of the white man!

Except for the northwest Indians who were fishermen and the Pueblo of the Southwest who farmed, the first Americans were primarily hunters and gathers. There were space and resources aplenty. There was no regional planning, no zoning, no building permits.

As for the native flora and fauna, to the north, west, and east, the land was predominately tall grass prairie and patches of hardwoods where the buffalo and gray wolf were major inhabitants. In the southern region, which bordered the Ozarks, the land was more broken with alternating patches of prairie and hardwoods. Within and along the edges of these areas were deer, elk, and bands of prairie chickens. Periodically feeding in the hardwoods and on rare occasions nesting were huge flocks of passenger pigeons. Ruffed grouse and ivory-billed woodpeckers were permanent residents. Also living in these woodsier areas were the black bear, cougar, and red wolf, the smaller cousin of the gray, as well as the native gray fox.

The big rivers and their smaller tributaries served as home and highway not only to the first Americans, but to furbearers such as the muskrat, beaver, and otter, and as flyways for ducks, geese, cranes, and songbirds.

The hollows found within the sycamores and cottonwoods that spread their branches along the edges of these streams provided excellent nesting habitat for the colorful Carolina parakeet. Laced among their branches were the huge, bulky nests of the southern bald eagle and the smaller, less conspicuous red-shouldered hawks. Nesting on the edges and working the drier open areas were the red-tailed hawks.

Modern historians have viewed the first Americans as basically environmentally friendly, and before the arrival of the Europeans that was true. Again, that's because with few exceptions they were primarily hunters and gathers living a subsistence life-style. There was limited time and economic reward for exploiting wildlife and other resources. But with the arrival of the Europeans, the indigenous culture was flooded with an array of new and mysterious wares. For beads, blankets, gunpowder, and brandy, the Indians eagerly traded their birthright — land and wildlife — in much the same way that we, today, trade clean air, water, our traditional social values, and communities, for the wares of modern industrial society. The common genetic seed of greed cuts to the bone, all the way

6

back to our human origins. A case in point: the Kaskaskia Indians left the Illinois River and immigrated to the River Des Peres in 1700 because of the increased encroachment of the Iroquois into their territory. This occurred because the Iroquois, who had traded furs to the Dutch and later the English, had wiped out the valuable furbearing animals in their own territory. And even before the arrival of the Europeans, it has been theorized that because of their hunting practices, the Indians were partially responsible for the disappearance of the woolly mammoths, mastodons, and perhaps several other big game species.

Kaskaskia Indian, 1790s, by General George-Victor Collot, from "Collot's Journey in North America."

2 - The Arrival of the Europeans

The Spanish, during their stay, spent most of their energy exploiting and then protecting the rich reserves of gold and silver they had taken from the Indians of Mexico and Central and South America. The English were the number one domesticators and cultivators on the North American continent. They had begun their settlements along the Atlantic seacoast, and it would take the frontiersmen, the ax, the ox, and the plow about a century and a half to reach the crest of the Appalachians. It was only then that they would seriously covet the Mississippi watershed.

THE FRENCH

During the mid to late 1600's, the three great European powers, England, France, and Spain, struggled for control of the North American continent. The French had the least impact on the local inhabitants and the native flora and fauna.

Unlike the English to the east, who were obsessed with the concept of private property and involved in a variety of industries requiring the subjugation of the land, wildlife, and the first Americans, the French concentrated their efforts on the fur trade. In so doing they came to value the Indians as trading partners and even bestowed French citizenship on them.

On April 9, 1682, following Joliet's and Father Marquette's discovery of the headwaters of the Mississippi in 1673, La Salle, who had descended the Mississippi to its mouth, claimed the entire Mississippi watershed for France. In 1762, nearing the end of the French and Indian War, Pierre Laclede and his partner Antoine Maxent were granted exclusive trading rights to the upper Mississippi River. The following winter, Laclede chose the high ground across from Cahokia as the site of his trading post, which he named St. Louis in honor of King Louis XV of France.

The number of French immigrating to America never came close to that of the English. Unlike farming and most of the other industries the English engaged in, the transient nature of the fur trade was not conducive to the traditional life-style of the French. Thus a large number of the Frenchmen involved in the fur trade often lived among the Indians and often married Indian women.

Another factor in their limited impact on the environment was that the French generally limited the amount of land an individual could own. The government granted trading rights to companies such as Maxent Laclede

& Co., who selected sites for trading posts. The government authorities would later lay out a town and grant each head of a family who was to reside there a lot varying in size from one to two arpents, an area a little over 0.85 of an acre. Occasionally, the government would issue a plot of land to a group who would subdivide it later.

In addition to these town lots, each family was granted ownership of a portion of the common field. In the St. Louis area, the average family received a section one arpent wide by forty arpents long, with larger families often receiving larger allotments. Common fields were situated on the best agricultural lands close to the settlement. These fields were usually enclosed with wooden fences to keep out domestic stock as well as wildlife. Each family not only was required to take care of their individual plots but shared in the construction of the fence. All issues related to the fields, such as the time of plowing, planting, and harvesting, were governed by law.

The commons was a much larger area than the common fields, usually several thousand acres, consisting of both woods and pasture. These lands were owned collectively by the community and not subdivided, as the common fields were. From the commons, wood was cut for fires and construction. These lands were also a place for livestock to forage.

The nearly 2,000 acres of Jefferson Barracks military post, founded in 1826, was part of the old Carondelet commons. It was sold by the local residents to the U. S. government for a five-dollar gold piece in the hope that a military post in the area would stimulate the local economy. The original community had been nicknamed Vide Poche meaning "empty pockets." Some historians believe the name reflected the local poverty. Others speculate that because horse racing and betting was an major attraction there, participants often left with empty pockets. Whatever the case, the Jefferson Barracks transaction has the distinction of being the cheapest land purchase ever made by the United States government.

Though it was not the case in all French settlements, farming in St. Louis and Carondelet was always secondary to the fur trade. Especially during the Spanish period, St. Louis often ran short of flour and on occasion had to import it from their more industrial neighbors in Ste. Genevieve. Thus, St. Louis, like Carondelet, received its own nickname — Paincourt, which in French means "short bread," referring to the fact that St. Louis was often short of bread.

In some ways, the farming practices of the French resembled those of the Indians. For example, although each family had its own individual plot, like the Indians, they farmed side by side. The French grew a greater variety of grains than the Indians, and a more significant difference was that they had domesticated stock. Hogs and cattle foraging in the commons began to destroy the forest understory, as cattle stripped the leaves and stems of small trees and bushes and the hogs dug up the roots. As the understory receded, so did the ruffed grouse and wild turkey, the black bear, cougar, and red wolf. Deer continued to be plentiful in the St. Louis area, but the elk, less able to tolerate human intrusion, had begun their retreat with the arrival of the first settlers. Nevertheless, the French minimized their impact on the native people, flora, and fauna by reserving most of their colonial holdings for the fur trade, clustering their people in towns, and restricting most local activities to the commons and common fields. As for transportation, there were crude dirt roads connecting major settlements such as Ste. Genevieve, Carondelet, and St. Louis, but as was the case with the Indians, the waterways served as the major highways to the traders and trappers.

The French controlled St. Louis from 1682 until November of 1762, when the west bank of the Great River was ceded to the Spanish in the secret Treaty of Fontainebleau.

Generally, when conflict broke out in Europe, France and Spain were allies against the British. When the French realized they were going to lose the French and Indian War (1754–1763) and their colonial holdings in America, they ceded the western half of the Mississippi watershed to Spain, hoping this would help to stop English expansion beyond the east bank of the river and enable them to later stake another claim to North America.

When word reached the French living on the east side that the Treaty of Paris had granted England the eastern half of the watershed, a number of French families moved across the river to St. Louis and Ste. Genevieve. By the time the Spanish actually took control of Louisiana, there were approximately fifty families living in St. Louis and several hundred in Ste. Genevieve. However, it wasn't until May 20, 1770, that the Spanish Lieutenant Governor Piernas arrived in St. Louis to take control of Upper Louisiana.

THE SPANISH

It was Hernando De Soto, a Spaniard, who in 1541 was the first European to see the Mississippi, thus giving his country the first European claim to its watershed. However, as previously mentioned, at that time Spain was primarily preoccupied with the gold and silver of Mexico. Their conquest of Mexico in 1521 and Peru in 1532 were to make Spain the most powerful country in Europe for the rest of the century. The downside for Spain was that its new-found wealth led to nearly a hundred years of relentless piracy that drained the country's treasury and culminated in war with England. After the defeat of the Spanish Armada in 1588, it was all down hill for Spain.

Though the Spanish were interested in Louisiana, as the western half of the watershed was then known, they first saw the acquisition as serving primarily as a buffer colony protecting their prize possession, Mexico, against foreign encroachment. In the early part of their rule, that meant keeping the English on the east side of the Mississippi. The problem with such a plan is that to have a effective buffer you must be able to protect your borders, and that required bodies.

In 1775 the Spanish government encouraged officials in Upper Louisiana to recruit French Canadians living on the east side to settle here. Few came. Most were poor and didn't have the resources to make the move. Thus, in 1778 the government offered immigrating families, in addition to free land grants, limited supplies of grain, livestock, and farming equipment to help them make it through their first season. The only stipulation was that the person must build on the property and cultivate the land within a year and a day of the grant. Again there were few takers. That same plan was eventually extended to include Spaniards back home as well as French, Italian, and German Catholics. Again the effort met with limited success.

Early on, the Spanish had problems with English traders encroaching on their territory and trading with the warring Osage Indians. The government countered by constructing a fort near the mouth of the Missouri, Fort Don Carlos. But the English traders found that once they slipped past the fort, they were home free.

In 1778, in an attempt to keep the Osage in check, the Spanish invited the Shawnee and Delaware, along with their trader Louis Lorimier, to settle on the west side of the river. These two tribes had sided with the French against the English in the French and Indian War and of course were no longer welcome in their own homeland, now English territory. The group first settled in the New Madrid area but moved to present-day Cape Girardeau, where in 1795 Lorimier was given land grant to the surrounding area.

During the American Revolution, 1775–1783, the Spanish followed the lead of their old allies the French by siding with the Americans. It was also during that war that the English engaged Emanuel Hess and Jean Marie Ducharme, fur traders, along with the Sac and the Fox and several other northern tribes, to attack St. Louis and Cahokia. At that time, due to the daring exploits of George Rogers Clark, Cahokia as well as most of the area to the east was under American occupation. To achieve their objective, Hess and Ducharme were to solicit the aid of the Chippewa, Northern Sioux, the Sac, and the Fox. In return for their efforts, both traders were promised a share of the Missouri River fur trade if they succeeded.

On May 26, 1780, over a thousand Indians swarmed down on St. Louis and Cahokia. Thanks to prior warning, the Spanish governor of Upper Louisiana, Fernando De Leyba, stationed in St. Louis, was able to put up a stone tower and trenches surrounding the city. De Leyba also received aid from a regiment of troops under Lieutenant Cartabona of Ste. Genevieve. Also responding to his call for help were local hunters and trappers, as well as George Rogers Clark, who would defend the East Side. These efforts paid off, and the British attack was repelled. Thus, St. Louis and the rest of Louisiana remained Spanish, and Cahokia and the area east of the river, known as the Northwest Territory, remained under American control.

The Treaty of Paris, signed September 3, 1783, recognized American Independence and set the boundary of the new country along the east side of the Great River. Had the previous attack on St. Louis and Cahokia succeeded, it's quite possible that the British would have regained control of the Northwest Territory, and the American-Canadian boundary at the end of the Revolutionary War would have been set along the Ohio River. In other words, East St. Louisans would be Canadians.

At that point, it was the American frontiersmen that the Spanish became nervous about. By the 1790's, Spain had realized that the price of trying to keep foreigners out of their territory was not cost-effective. That realization came down hard in the year 1795, when the Spanish officials in Upper Louisiana learned first of Pinckney's Treaty, granting the United States free navigation on the Mississippi, and then that their country was once again at war with England.

Thus, in 1796 the Spanish authorities in America revised their policy and opened the western bank to American settlement. It was their hope that the new settlers would help to repulse future British attacks. With an offer of free land and no taxes, the floodgates were opened, and within a few years, Americans made up the majority of the residents in Upper Louisiana.

Among the Americans who took up the Spanish offer was Daniel Boone, who followed his son Daniel Morgan Boone to Missouri in 1799. Boone was 64 at the time and was given a grant of 1,000 arpents of land in the Femme Osage valley in what is today St. Charles County. Boone was appointed a syndic, which is similar to a magistrate judge. Though he would lose the title to the land after the American take-over, a special act of Congress later confirmed it. It was there that he lived out the rest of his days, until his death at the age of 86 in 1820.

Even before Spain's new policy was implemented, new settlements had cropped up. In 1768, the French Canadian Louis Blanchette founded St. Charles 21 miles upstream from the mouth of the Missouri. At the time it was called Les Petites Cotes (the little hills). As it does today, the new town drew residents from the St. Louis area. Hunters came because of the fresh, relatively untapped supply of game. The farmers came because of the productive bottom lands. By 1800, the village had over 600 residents.

In 1785, a small group of Creoles from St. Louis, Cahokia, and Kaskaskia could be found working the common fields in the Coldwater

Creek area about 15 miles northwest of St. Louis. This became the village of St. Ferdinand, today known as Florissant. By 1800 its population reached nearly 300. Other settlements sprang up in and around the St. Louis area. The Village of Marais des Liards was founded just west of Florissant in 1794 by Robert Owens. In 1800, its population exceeded 200. By the time the area was transferred to the United States in 1804, Americans had become the majority. It was they who eventually changed the name of the settlement to Bridgeton.

As the Spanish era drew to a close, the population growth of St. Louis and Carondelet not only slowed but at times actually declined. Former residents often sold their town lots and strip farms to new arrivals and speculators and headed for greener pastures, particularly St. Charles and Florissant, where once again the land was free and game seemed fatter and more plentiful. As for the American frontiersman, they weren't into communal working and living. They were rugged individualists who, like Boone, wanted lots of elbow room and lots of land.

THE FRENCH, ONE MORE TIME

Following France's defeat by the British in 1798, Napoleon turned his attention to America where he dreamed of creating a new French Empire. In the Treaty of San Ildefonso, October 1, 1800, a deal with the Spanish was struck. Napoleon agreed to place the Prince of Parma, son-in-law of the Spanish king, on the newly erected throne of Etruria, and Spain returned Louisiana to France. With that, Spanish officials in American must have breathed a huge sigh of relief.

Napoleon had plans to use the Island of Haiti as his base of operation from which to advance his dream of a colonial empire in the West Indies and Louisiana. But the black uprising started there by Toussaint L. Ouverture several years earlier was again renewed. The revolution, along with an outbreak of yellow fever, would cost Napoleon 50,000 men and put his dream on hold. Then came the new threat of war with Great Britain and Napoleon's pressing need for money.

These disturbing developments induced Napoleon to sell not only New Orleans to the Americans, as they had requested, but the whole of Louisiana. In a treaty signed April 30, 1803, for fifteen million dollars, the U. S. government acquired all of Louisiana. However, it wasn't until March 9 and 10, 1804, that Upper Louisiana was officially transferred first back to the French and then to the Americans at St. Louis. Thus, on the 10th of March, for the first time, the American flag flew on both sides of the river. By then three-fifths of the inhabitants in St. Louis and surrounding area were Americans.

THE AMERICANS

With the American take-over, residents in the area who had previously received Spanish land grants became greatly concerned. Two major problems existed. First, most residents of Upper Louisiana who had received legal grants before October 1, 1800, the date Spain returned the land back to France, had not properly filed their deeds, which had to be done in New Orleans. Second, there was the question of whether or not the new U. S. government would recognize those grants issued after the above date. The issue of land titles would dominate local politics up to and beyond the time of statehood.

In the meantime, land speculation became rampant. Many prominent residents such as the Chouteaus, James Mackay, and others bought up as many of the old land grants as they could get their hands on. They were aware that it would be some time before the U. S. government would auction off any of its new land, for it first had to be surveyed and then broken down into townships and sections. Meanwhile, the flood of Americans continued.

3 - Missouri: Territory to Statehood

President Jefferson had proposed that Upper Louisiana be temporarily closed to new settlement until the remaining lands across the river in the Northwest Territory were fully occupied. To achieve this goal, he wanted to negotiate treaties removing the remaining eastern tribes west of the Great River. It was his hope that by the time the Northwest Territory was settled, the Indians would be better prepared for the advance of American states westward.

But Congress and the American frontiersmen had a mind of their own. In 1804, Congress drew a line across Louisiana along the 33rd parallel. The area to the south would be called the District of Orleans, and the area to the north, which included St. Louis, the District of Louisiana. Of great concern to the local residents was that all land grants issued after October 1, 1800, were considered null and void. Well, at least for the time being.

Under the law of the District of Louisiana, St. Louis was to be governed by the officials of the Territory of Indiana. Local residents strongly protested. In response to their protest, Congress in 1805 turned the district into a first-class territory and made St. Louis the capital. However, as was the case under the Spanish, all government officials were appointed. Under the provisions of the old Ordinance of 1787, Missouri began its slow movement towards statehood. In 1812, the territory had over 5,000 free white males of voting age, which allowed Congress to elevate it to a second-class territory. With its new classification, the territory was renamed the Territory of Missouri. This allowed the residents to elect representatives to a territorial House of Representatives. The upper house of the legislature and the Territorial Governor, however, were still appointed by the President.

In 1816 The Missouri Territory was advanced to a third-class status, which allowed it to elect both houses of the territorial legislature. The following year the population of the area reached the 60,000 mark — the magic number required to begin petitioning Congress for statehood. A petition was presented to Congress in 1818, and in December of that year a bill for statehood was introduced. However, due to the nagging slavery issue, it wasn't until March 6, 1820, following the passage of the Missouri Compromise engineered by Henry Clay, that an enabling act was passed and signed by President Monroe.

On June 12, 1820, the Missouri Constitution Convention began in St. Louis, and on July 19, they adopted a constitution. As permitted under the

Missouri Compromise, the new constitution protected the institution of slavery. On August 28, 1820, the first state election was held. A governor, a lieutenant governor, a representative to Congress, and members of the state legislature were chosen. On October 2, the newly elected General Assembly picked their two United States senators. They were David Barton and Thomas H. Benton. It should be noted here that it wasn't until the passage of the seventeenth amendment to the U. S. Constitution in 1913 that United States senators were elected directly by the people.

Missourians now felt they had met the conditions set forth by Congress. However, when Missouri congressmen arrived in Washington, they were not seated due to a controversial provision in the new state constitution pertaining to former slaves. Finally, after much debate and compromise, again thanks to Henry Clay, President Monroe on August 10, 1821, officially declared Missouri the twenty-fourth state of the Union.

Under the Missouri Constitution, counties are laid out by the state legislature, and all cities are considered creatures of the state. That is, the state constitution lays out the guidelines for becoming a city. As of 1995, Missouri has had four constitutions. The most recent was approved in 1945.

As previously mentioned, up until 1876, what is today St. Louis City and St. Louis County were a single political unit. In that year, because of continual bickering between the rural and urban areas, the state legislature allowed the two to split. Thus — I know this is confusing — St. Louis City is considered both a city and a county. That is, it has the powers of a county as well as the rights and privileges of an incorporated area.

STATE MOTTO, SYMBOLS, SONG, AND NAME

Missouri's official motto is *Salus populi suprema lex estro* (Let the welfare of the people be the supreme law). But Missouri is best known by its nickname which is "The Show Me State," which became popular nationally in 1899 when our Congressman Willard Vandiver in Philadelphia said, "I'm from Missouri, and you'll have to show me."

Historians have researched this expression and have come up with a number of suggestions for its origin. Perhaps the best interpretation goes that back to the gold mining days in Colorado. After the placer gold had played out and people were digging for gold, a lot of miners from Missouri went to Colorado to find work. Most of them had no experience in that type of mining. So, after a man was hired, the foreman was told, "He's from Missouri and you'll have to show him." So, instead of "Show me" meaning prove it to me," it's more likely that "Show me" means "teach me."

In 1923, the state legislature chose as our state flower the hawthorn, a scrubby bush of a tree with tiny nondescript flowers. Then in 1955, the

16

dogwood, which in early spring has large showy flowers, many times the size of the hawthorn's, was picked as our state tree. No one, of course, would complain about the bluebird being named the state bird. It was a great choice — after all, it's one of the few birds spirited enough to sing even in the winter.

No one objected when galena was named our state mineral (1967), the crinoid the state fossil (1989), and the black walnut our state nut (1990). Galena is a dark gray metallic lead sulfide mineral, the chief ore of lead. Rich deposits of galena just south of St. Louis made Missouri the world's largest producer of lead. The crinoid, also called the "sea lily," is a mineralized sea animal related to the starfish, which flourished in the ocean that covered this area over 250 million years ago. Because of their long, stem-like bodies that were once attached to the ocean floor and their flower-like tops, they can easily be mistaken for plants. Seldom is the entire fossil found. What's usually found are scattered disk-shaped body segments with round or star-shaped centers. The Indians often strung these and wore them as beads.

Also in 1967, mozarkite was named the state rock. Mozarkite is a beautifully banded variety of chert (flint) found mostly in the Ozarks. It is made up of various mottled shades of red or pink, which may be mixed with bands of white or gray. The First Americans made beautiful spear points and arrowheads from them. The one and only spear point I ever found in my yard as a child was a three-and-a-half-inch point made from pink mozarkite.

Then there's the case of the state insect. The leading contender for some time was the ladybug — until it was pointed out that it was a Japanese import (whoops!). In 1985 the legislators finally settled on the ever-popular honeybee. Actually, like the ladybug, the honeybee is not a native Missourian. The English introduced the honeybee along the Atlantic coast around 1650. It did so well that, like the red fox, it preceded the frontiersmen westward by several seasons. Neither the honeybee or the red fox were common to the state until around 1800. The Indians even dubbed the honeybee the "white man's fly." An Osage legend says that on the first day the honeybee reached an Osage village, the Indians had a day of mourning. My personal favorites for the title of state insect would have been the tick or the chigger, and anyone who has met them on a personal level would have to agree that in spite of their size, they have a way of making their presence known. They are both native and found throughout the state and are among the most laid back of insects. They spend most of their time just lounging around waiting for an opportunity to drop-in on some unsuspecting host — the worst kind of uninvited quest.

The state government doesn't seem to know when to quit — now it's considering a state animal. Ever since trade was introduced between Missouri and Mexico by way of the Santa Fe Trail, the mule has been associated with our state. Over the years, it's actually become our unofficial symbol. But now that it's time to nail it down, there is something of a political issue. Some Republicans feel that the mule would be giving symbolic support to the Democratic party. Then, too, the mule is not only sterile but is a cross between an ass and a mare.

Thanks to Harry Truman, in 1949 the Missouri Waltz was named the official state song. It's a pretty tune although the lyrics aren't politically correct by today's standards.

Now, the really big issue: what is the correct pronunciation of Missouri? Is it Missou-rah or Missou-ree? This question has divided Missourians more than any other issue since the Civil War. No blood has been shed over this question, but a hard cold war goes on with no truce in sight. Even though a number of doctoral theses have been published on the subject, there is no general agreement among the scholars.

Things really heated up during the 1986 national election. When President Reagan came to our state to endorse Republican candidates, he used the Missou-ree pronunciation. The problem was, the candidate he was endorsing, Kit Bond, was a Missou-rah man. Bond won against Harriet Woods, who agreed with the President — perfect example of modern-day political gridlock. The Missou-ree group said a president should outrank a senator, right? The Missou-rah faction caucused a while, and then in a brilliant political move conceded. Yes, a president should outrank a senator, they agreed. President Truman, a native Missourian, they pointed out, always said Missou-rah. See what I mean!

Following that 1986 election, I pondered the question and asked myself how I could bring an end to this madness. I came up with the following song, which should put the question to rest once and for all.

MISSOURI?

Is it Missou-rah, or Missou-ree ?
What should it be?
What the heck's all the shoutin' about?
Some say it's Missou-rah
Others say Missou-ree.
But I say misery
When I'm feeling down and out.

If you're in Columbia, Mo., and the team scores
And the game becomes a rout
Its Missou-rah Missou-rah . . . Rah, Rah, Rah!

But if you're on that lazy river west of the Shenandoah
Or doin' that pretty waltz
It's Missou -ou-ou-ou-ree.

But when the crops fail,
Next it's winds and hail,
Then it's too darn hot,
Then you're livin' in a state of Misery.

So you see!
It can be Missou-rah, Missou-ree
once in awhile a little Misery.
But most of the time
It's not a bad place to be.
Yes, it's home sweet home to me.
Missou-rah-ah-ee.

* * *

19

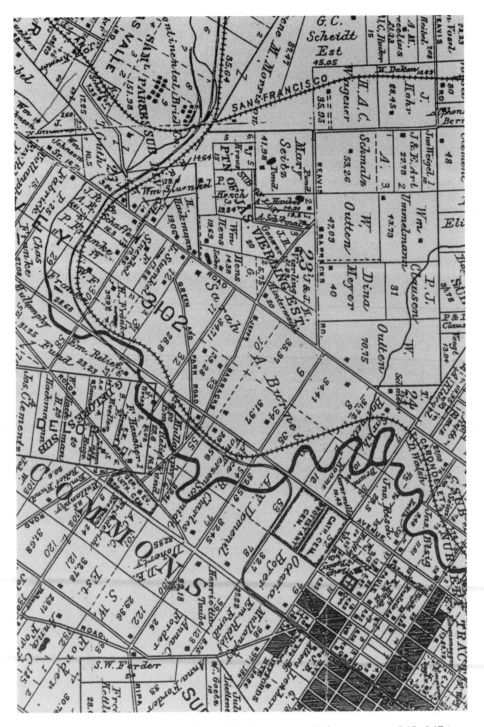

Gravois Creek land survey, pre-1930. (See map and photos on pp. 145–147.)

PART II

ROOTED

I immediately procured a horse and started for the country, taking no baggage with me, of course. There is an insignificant creek — the Gravois — between Jefferson Barracks and the place to which I was going, and at that day there was not a bridge over it from its source to its mouth . . . . I found the banks full to overflowing, and the current rapid . . . . So I struck into the stream, and in an instant the horse was swimming and I being carried down by the current. I headed the horse towards the other bank and soon reached it, wet through and without other clothes on that side of the stream. I went on, however, to my destination and borrowed a dry suit from my — future — brother-in-law. We were not of the same size, but the clothes answered every purpose until I got more of my own.

— U.S. Grant on his way to White Haven to propose to Julia Dent before joining his regiment just prior to the outbreak of the Mexican War. From the Personal Memoirs of U.S. Grant, May, 1844.

21

4 - Two Families and a Place

GERMAN IMMIGRATION

I was born on June 22, 1941, in St. Louis County, in the Gravois Creek watershed. At that time the area was still mostly rural. My mother's folks were all descendants of German truck farmers who began working the creek bottom at the time of the Civil War. Carl Franke (1837–1922) came to America from Todtenhausen, a small town near Minden, West Germany, at the age of twenty, which would be sometime between late 1857 and 1858. We know little about the family's background but we can trace their roots back to a home recorded in the town records as early as 1682. We also know that tens of thousands of other Germans had already come to and passed through St. Louis. One man in particular helped to send them in that direction. His name was Gottfried Duden.

Duden was a wealthy lawyer and public official of Mulheim on the Ruhr who came to Missouri in the fall of 1824. He was traveling across the country in search of a place for his overcrowded countrymen to settle. From St. Louis, he traveled up the Missouri River fifty miles into Warren County, where he acquired a farm which he worked for several years. In 1827 he returned to Germany. In 1829 he published his popular *Report of a Journey to the Western States of North America*. In his report he romantically compared the topography and fertility of the Missouri River country to that of the Rhineland. Best of all, he pointed out that the land was plentiful and cheap. Not only did Duden encourage Germans to come and settle in Missouri, but his book gave detailed instructions on how to do it. In 1830, there were fewer than twenty German families living in St. Louis. Duden, more than any other individual, helped to change that.

In 1833, following a failed revolt, the Gieszen Emigration Society was formed in Hesse by Friedrich Muench and Paul Follenius — both had read Duden's report. Thus, in that year they brought seven hundred Germans to St. Louis. Though most had come to acquire farms in the Missouri River valley, by the time they reached St. Louis many had exhausted their funds and chose to stay in and around the city. In 1836, the German Settlement Society of Philadelphia also decided to take Duden's advice and acquired 1,300 acres of land in the Gasconade River valley. There they built the town of Hermann, which was to become their base of operation for developing other communities.

In 1839, 600 Saxons settled fifty miles south of St. Louis in Perry

County. They were conservative Lutherans who were motivated as much by the desire for religious freedom as they were for land. Out of this group were 120 individuals who decided to live in St. Louis where they founded Trinity Lutheran Church. In Perry County, the group organized what was to become the Lutheran Church Missouri Synod — today the largest group of Lutherans in the country. There they also founded the first coeducational college in the state, Concordia Seminary. In 1849, the Seminary was moved to St. Louis. In addition to the above groups, a number of German Catholics settled in the city.

As a rule, most of these early Germans were conservative and pretty much blended into the landscape. When possible, they preferred developing their own communities where they could live in tightly knit family and community units, and where they could continue their German heritage. Once settled, they sank their roots deep, and unlike the typical American frontiersman, they tended to stay put.

However, by the end of the decade, a new breed of Germans was arriving. In Europe, 1848 was known as the "Year Of Revolution." In that year there were food shortages, recession, and rising nationalism leading to general unrest. In February, the citizens in France overthrew King Louis Philippe and set up the Second French Republic under Napoleon II. In March, revolution spread to Austria, and it wasn't long until riots broke out in Berlin. In Germany, an attempt to overthrow the throne of Prussia had failed, and for those involved it was a good time to leave Germany. Between 1848 and 1850 over 35,000 Germans arrived in St. Louis, and by 1860 there were over 50,000 German-born citizens living in what today is St. Louis City and County. Suddenly, almost overnight, they became the largest ethnic group in the area. These new arrivals were known as the 48ers.

Though many of the Germans who had preceded them were as well educated as the 48ers, they were quieter and slow to respond to nativist contempt. Not so the 48ers. Though they had lost the battle abroad, they were still true libertarians, freethinkers, and reformers. They were not only for reforming the churches and the schools but also for ending the institution of slavery. They were also highly cultured and did much to advance theater, literature, music, and other arts. In 1850, the first Turnverein (Turner Society) was formed in St. Louis. Not only did these societies aid new immigrants, they also served as cultural centers that promoted political liberty. They were coeducational, and in addition to providing gymnasiums, they maintained schools, libraries, put on plays, promoted festivals and other community functions. In time, they primarily became social clubs and recreational centers, somewhat like the modern-day YMCA. In short, it didn't take the 48ers long to make their presence known in St. Louis.

Other than being anti-slavery, their views didn't set well with the earlier Germans — Lutherans, Methodists, and Catholics, who were to become their greatest critics. Soon St. Louis Germans were divided into two distinct groups — the Grays who preceded the 48ers, and the 48ers, who were called the Greens. Each group had their own German newspaper through which they traded barbs.

Meanwhile, back in Europe, the Crimean War erupted in 1854, and there was an increased movement towards German unification. Thus, there were still lots of reasons for a young man like Carl Franke to consider coming to America.

Of all the reasons for folks to came to Missouri and St. Louis, be they French, Spanish, German, or American frontiersmen, right up there at the top of the list, as always, was economic opportunity. And if you wanted to be a farmer, you needed land. While America had a vast frontier, Europe, long before the mid-1800's, had been almost entirely domesticated and cultivated. What wild lands remained were owned by noble families or the Crown. Throughout Europe, the system known as primogeniture had been institutionalized under the law. This required that the firstborn son of each family inherit all his father's property. Though this seems harsh, it prevented land holdings from being broken down into smaller and smaller units to the point where they would be of little value. Under that system, any other sons had to take up some kind of craft or trade or become common laborers in the cities. As for the daughters, they might receive a dowry upon marriage, but their husbands, of course, were to provide for them.

THE FRANKE FAMILY

We do not know all the reasons Carl Franke decided to come to America, but one thing for sure is that he wanted to own his own land and become a farmer. I've been told that he arrived in Carondelet by way of Ellis Island and is believed to have passed through Pennsylvania, then went down the Ohio River and up the Mississippi. At the time St. Louis was infamous for its cholera epidemics, which often entered the city via the river. Though 1857–58 was relatively cholera-free, steamboats rumored to have infected passengers were often turned away. Perhaps this is how Carl Franke ended up in Carondelet instead of St. Louis. Whatever, the story goes that once he got here, he followed a man carrying a Bible into a church, where he was surprised to meet a relative from back home. It is believed that he must have lived and worked in the Carondelet area sometime before the outbreak of the American Civil War.

Missouri, as previously mentioned, was a slave state, and the governor in 1861 was Claiborne F. Jackson, both a southerner and a secessionist. While the governor was preparing to take the state out of the Union, Congressman Francis (Frank) P. Blair, Jr., of St. Louis was just as

24

Elizabeth Meyer Franke.

Carl Franke.

determined not to let it happen. It is generally agreed that it was he, as much as any single individual, and the Germans in the St. Louis area, more than any other ethnic group, who kept the state in the union. Thus, Carl Franke in 1861 joined the Missouri Guard and, like the other Germans, fought for the Union. At last the Grays and the Greens had a common cause. They put aside their differences and marched off together to save the Union and end slavery.

It is believed that shortly after the Civil War, Carl owned and worked land in the Lemay area near the River Des Peres. I was told that he acquired this land from the government in lieu of a pension before moving to the Gravois Creek area just south of Green Park Road in what is today Mehlville. At that time much of the surrounding area was still considered part of the old Carondelet commons.

Carl married Elizabeth Meyer (1838–1897) in 1861, most likely just prior to joining the Army. Elizabeth was from Ellringhausen, Westphalia Germany. It is recorded that she came to St. Louis by way of New Orleans in June of 1860. But that is all we know about her past. Carl and Elizabeth had four sons and three daughters — Henry, William, Elizabeth, Caroline, Peter, Louis (Louie), and Julia.

Henry (1865–1945), their firstborn, was my grandfather. We know very little about his youth other than the fact that when he was fourteen he was sent to school somewhere in St. Louis. The following is one of two letters we know he wrote to his parents during this period:

St. Louis Jan. 1, 1879

Dear Parents,

Just as the brook murmurs and waves come rolling till the brook flows on into the river and then into the sea to find its rest, so does the life of one generation to another fade away, mixed with luck and unluck, till we pass to eternity. And now at New Years we stand happy and full of joy and thinking of the many good gifts that have come to us in the passed year and on this day dear parents I feel that I should thank yous for all the good that you have done for me dear parents, for that you have sent me to the city to school and now that I could help work you send me to town to school that I should have an education. And what can I do for you? Only give you my childish will to do my best and study real hard and be good and give you pleasure.

So I will try my best to study and to be good. Today on this day I will bring yous my New Year wish and wishing yous a happy New Year and that God may let us live to see many more happy ones. Hoping that this childish wish makes you happy and surprising you, I am your loving son.

Heinrich Franke

No one knows what school he went to or how long he attended. We do know that he did return to the creek bottom and, like his father, married and became a successful farmer. His first wife was Emma Bollmann (1871–1897) from Quincy, Illinois, whose family owned the property at the northwest corner of Lemay Ferry and Will Avenue. They were married November 12, 1891, and their only child Charles (Collie) was born on January 26, 1896. A year and a half later on December 6, 1897, Emma died. The cause of death was unknown, but family members believe it was either food poisoning or appendicitis. For Henry 1897 was a difficult year; in November his mother Elizabeth also passed away. It is said that his younger sister Julia helped him raise Charles until he married Amelia Meyer (1878–1941), my grandmother, on March 9, 1898.

Amelia's father, Frederick, came to America from Germany in 1663 and joined his brother who owned a farm across the river somewhere in Illinois. Like Carl Franke he fought on the side of the Union during the Civil War. In 1864, he joined Company H of the Fiftieth Regiment of the Illinois Infantry and eventually served under General Sherman. He was wounded during the war and later received a pension of thirty dollars a month. Following the war Frederick also ended up in the Gravois Creek watershed, in the Affton area, where, like Carl, he eventually took up truck farming. In later years his property was acquired by the Affton Brickyard. Because of the poor road conditions in the County, like the Carl Franke family, Frederick attended the Carondelet Evangelical Church where he eventually meet and married Maria Krueger. The Meyers had six children — Caroline, Amelia, Mary, Louis, John, and Emma.

It was also at the Carondelet church that Henry Franke most likely first meet and then married Amelia. Henry and Amelia had seven daughters and two sons: Harry, Irene, Mary (Mamie), Oscar, Ella, Lillian, Florence, Mildred, and Agnes. My mother Agnes was born in 1916 on the 136th anniversary of the Battle of St. Louis, May 26. All of her sisters and brothers, with the exception of Charles, lived out most of their lives within a few miles of the Franke homestead. Charles was 21 years old when the U. S. entered World War I. The story goes that shortly thereafter, several of his uncles showed up at Henry Franke's home and took him to Winfield, Missouri, where he worked on the family farm where they raised wheat. Apparently there was a labor shortage during the war, and at the time wheat farmers were exempt from the draft.

After the war, Charles decided to stay in Winfield. I've been told that he preferred wheat farming to working on his knees as a truck farmer. In later years, he took up dairy farming. Mom's other two brothers, Harry and Oscar, stayed on in the creek bottom and eventually received equal shares of their father's land. Both brothers at best had a fourth or fifth grade education, but that didn't limit their curiosity and many interests. Oscar had a great interest in natural history. During his youth this big-boned man with huge hands collected and mounted butterflies. He loved to hunt, and like his cousin Art Franke, he learned taxidermy. They both developed reputations as the best taxidermists in the area. Some of Oscar's and Art's mounts and specimen cases might still be found in local taverns. Both Harry and Oscar were also avid readers.

Harry became interested in Indian lore and artifacts as well as antique firearms. In his youth, he collected artifacts on the family farm. Later he bought and traded not only Indian artifacts but guns. By the time he reached middle age, it is said that he had one of the most extensive private collections of Indian relics and antique firearms in the St. Louis area. He

27

and two other individuals were the original founders of the St. Louis Archaeological Society.

I loved visiting Uncle Harry and Aunt Olivia, for the wall of their screened-in porch was covered with antique guns. Strewn around the edges of the porch was an array of antiques, and next to the kitchen door leaned Harry's huge Sharp's buffalo rifle, which for sometime outweighed me. In their living room were display cases filled from top to bottom with what the family called his "Indian rocks." Uncle Harry always had time to show us kids his collection.

Like his brother, Oscar also collected antiques. But most of all, like their father and grandfather, they were truck farmers. Of all the types of farming I can think of, truck farming has got to be the most back-breaking and labor-intense.

LIFE IN THE GRAVOIS CREEK AREA

The truck farmers of the area grew every type of vegetable the land could produce. They hauled their produce to the city where they sold them to retailers at Produce Row at the corner of Third Street and Broadway. In addition to vegetables they grew a little hay, harvested some fruit, raised hogs and fowl, and kept at least one milk cow. In the early days, they worked their fields with mules and horses.

In their spare time, these farm boys hunted the fields, forest, and creek, adding wild game to their family's diet, and in so doing gained their own personal sense of pride. By then all the big game, including deer, were gone. So, of course, were the grouse and prairie chickens. But the clearing of the land for both row crops and pasture provided great habitats for rabbits and quail. The remaining wooded areas also held a stable population of squirrels. As more and more woodlots were reduced in size, the gray squirrels began to outnumber the fox squirrels, who preferred the deeper woods.

In addition to hunting, the young men trapped furbearing animals at the edges of the fields, in and along the banks of the creek. They would rise before first light to run their trapline so they were sure to be back by breakfast and ready for their morning chores. The beaver were long gone, but the creek still produced a large number of muskrats ("musrats," as my uncles called them). They also trapped opossum, skunk, raccoon, and a few red and gray fox. As more and more land was cleared for crops and pasture, the red fox gradually began to outnumber the woodsier grays.

In addition to the German families working the Gravois Creek watershed, there were a number of Italian families. Both German and Italian families were neighborly and shared a strong sense of community. The Italian families were Catholic, while the German families were predominately Protestant. When the roads improved, my grandfather's family

28

became members of St. John's Evangelical and Reform Church founded in 1838 at what today is the northwest corner of Union Road and Lindbergh in South County. And at that site on October 15, 1840, the Evangelical Synod of North America was founded. Thereafter the church became the St. John's Evangelical and Reform Church and in later years became a member of the United Church of Christ.

Several of my mother's older brothers and sisters were teenagers in the 1920's. That was the Prohibition era, and a few of the enterprising locals found it profitable to convert a portion of their corn crop into bootleg whiskey. The wooded areas that bordered Gravois Creek were a perfect place for such operations. My Aunt Mildred told me that on certain days when the wind was right, they could get a good whiff of brew as they worked their fields.

In general, the local authorities looked the other way — it was the Feds you had to watch out for. According to the stories my uncles told me, the local sheriff would ride out on his motorcycle to warn the brewmasters of any planned bust. Occasionally, for PR purposes, a bust was staged. An old still no longer in use would be set up. The next day the papers would have a photo of a beat-up still and some down-on-his-luck local who was paid to take the rap. By the time the papers had been circulated the next day, the local was out of jail, and the smell of fresh brew was once again rising from the creek bottoms.

As was the case with most waste products, the refuse from the still was dumped directly into the creek. There it was fed upon by carp and other rough fish, which quickly became intoxicated.

Occasionally a real bust was made. Once, a large tank containing several hundred gallons of whisky was found across the creek from my Grandpa Franke's farm. It was blown up, and its contents quickly made its way into the creek. On that day, from that point and all the way to its confluence with the River Des Peres, thousands of fish floundered about in a drunken stupor. As the word got out, local farmers and townsfolk descended on the creek and scooped the fish up by the gunnysackful.

In 1933 Prohibition ended, and we were in the depths of the Great Depression. For those who worked in St. Louis and neighboring towns, it was a very difficult time. For my mother's family, however, as with many of the neighboring farmers, it was no more than a mild inconvenience. Actually, my mother's family prospered.

The least fortunate of the area often looked to the creek for relief. Many of the old-timers have told me that if it wasn't for the abundance of crawfish in the creek, they would have nearly starved. If there is any one thing that Gravois Creek was famous for in those early days, and even up until the time I was growing up, it was its crawfish.

In many ways, the life of the early truck farmers was only about a step and a half removed from that of the Indians and early French settlers. All three groups farmed and raised a variety of crops. Unlike most big-time farmers and ranchers today, they weren't dependent on a single cash crop or any one source of income. Thus, like the Indians, they were quite adaptable to the fickle whims of both humans and nature.

While truck farmers didn't work communal food plots like the Indians or practice strip farming like the French, when possible they clustered together in family units. In the ways of the Old World farmers, fathers and sons worked side by side. Unlike in "the old country," many farmers here were able to acquire enough land so that they could divide it among most if not all of their sons. For example, my great grandfather Carl bought the parcel of property his grandson Charles had inherited from his mother and then passed it on to his youngest son Louie. He paid well over the market value so that his grandson would have a little nest egg of his own.

By the time my mother entered high school Grandpa Henry had retired from farming. In 1929 he built a new brick bungalow closer to Green Park Road, and Uncle Henry and Aunt Olivia and Uncle Oscar and Aunt Edna took over the old home and worked the farm together. Grampa also had a new home built nearby for his in-laws — Frederick and Maria Meyer. After their passing Uncle Oscar and Aunt Edna moved there and raised their family. Unlike modern families of today, many of the farmers, like the Franke's, were able to hold together as an extended family from cradle to grave. Such things as Medicare and nursing homes were unknown and unthinkable.

Most important of all, perhaps, like the Indians and French before them, they were not only close to one another, they were equally close to the land and in tune with its seasonal cycles. There was something very special, even spiritual, about eating the food they raised, harvested, dug up, fished and hunted for. Both boys and girls grew up with a strong sense of their place in relation to the landscape, their clan, their individual family unit, their religion, and their community. As they matured, boys were trained by their fathers, girls by their mothers, and both experienced well-defined rites of passage. By the time they reached adulthood, they really knew they were men and women. For better or worse, there was no confusion as to their identity and their responsibilities to self, family, and community. In these ways, over the millenniums, not much had changed in the creek bottom. One noticeable difference between them and most of those that preceded them was that they built permanent communities. They were rooted — well, at least for awhile.

*Frederick and
Maria Kruger Meyer.*

*The Franke / Meyer Clan (photo from front cover).
L–R: Children — Florence Franke, Agnes Franke (Mom), Mildred Franke.
Standing: Lillie Meyer, Grandma and Grandpa Franke, Sophia and Louie
Meyer, Lizzi and John Meyer, Great-grandma Meyer.*

Photos from top to bottom:

Top: Henry Franke's first home off Green Park Road. Note: summer house to right was used for cooking.

Center: L–R: Irene Franke, Lillie Franke, Mildred Franke, Carl Franke, Henry Franke. Standing: Mamie Jacobson

Bottom: Agnes Franke Taylor (Mom)

THE TAYLOR FAMILY

The above way of life was good for three complete generations of Frankes. My mom's was the last. It was my generation who lived between two worlds as the land — at first gradually, then all of a sudden — was transformed from a predominately rural to a suburban area. It began when folks like my dad's family began moving there from the city. They came primarily not to live and work, like those who preceded them, but to "reside."

Actually, Grampa Taylor was something of an exception. His family roots went all the way back to pre-Revolutionary Pennsylvania. His father Zachary Taylor (1847–1939), the youngest of five children, was born at Reading, Pennsylvania, the son of William and Rebecca Taylor. His mother died when he was six, and his father died two years later. Following his father's death, he went to live with his Uncle John Taylor in Northumberland, Pennsylvania. He attended the Poughkeepsie Business College in New York, after which he returned to Northumberland, where he taught for several years. He next worked in the business world for several more years. But what he liked to do best was hunt and fish, and Pennsylvania was getting crowded. He wanted to see the prairie and hunt prairie chickens, so in 1880, at the age of thirty-three he grabbed his gun and headed west to what was then the edge of civilization — Topeka, Kansas. There for the next five years, he worked as an auditor for the Santa Fe Railroad and began checking out prime hunting and fishing areas. It didn't take him long to discover the Flint Hills and the Cottonwood River that ran through it.

Zachary's firstborn was my father's dad Roy Richie Taylor (1888–1968), a Kansas boy who, after completing several years of study in business and accounting at Baker University, moved to St. Louis in the early 1900's to earn his fortune. He first worked for Laclede Gas but quit because he questioned some of their business practices. The very next day he went to work as a bookkeeper at Commercial Foundry in Carondelet. At the time, the company was operating in the red. According to my Uncle Warren, it didn't take Grampa long to figure out that the factory foreman was stealing the company blind. The problem was that the foreman found out that Grampa knew it.

As usual, Grampa was in his office early one morning working on the books when the front door opened. It was the foreman with an iron weight, the kind used back then to draw open and close windows. He approached Grampa and said, "Taylor, I'm gonna get ya." By the time he got the words out, Grampa, who was somewhat short but powerful, had jumped over the desk and laid the man out cold on the floor. Moments later the back door opened. It was the foreman's son, also armed with an iron weight. He too bit the dust in short order. Grampa walked out of the

33

Photos from top to bottom:

Top: Zachary Taylor.

Center: Edith Drake Taylor.

Bottom: Sisters and brothers. L–R: Mabel, Harold, Roy and Helen.

office and sat down on the curb. Shortly, the company president arrived and asked Grampa what the problem was. Grampa said he was quitting and that the foreman and his son could be found on the office floor.

"Just a minute, Taylor," the president said. He went inside then came back out in a few minutes and asked Grampa how he'd like to be vice-president. Grampa had confirmed what he had suspected. Now, there is a true story about fighting your way to the top of the corporate ladder, literally.

Soon Grampa was head of the sales department, and with the graft cleaned up, the company began to prosper. Buying up all the company stock he could, Grampa quickly acquired 49 percent, the same amount as the president. (A local priest owned the remaining two percent.)

When the Depression struck, Grampa worked overtime to keep the company's head above water. Apparently, he didn't think the president was doing his part, and being in charge of the payroll, he decided to cut the salary not only of the president but of the president's daughter, who also worked for the company. Because he felt he was the one keeping the company afloat, he believed he was earning his pay — thus, no cut in his own salary. Well, you can imagine the president's reaction. With neither man holding a majority of the company stock, it became a stand-off. When the old priest died, the president bought the remaining two percent, giving him the fifty-one percent majority he needed to get rid of Grampa. On the day Grampa was fired, he told the president that he was making a big mistake and promised him that within a year the company would fold.

Grampa immediately went to work for the East St. Louis Casting Company across the river, and he took all his old customers with him except one. That single business was the one contract that Commercial had been losing money on.

Some months later my uncle was present when the Commercial Foundry president came to my grandfather's home, got down on his hands and knees, and begged him to come back. No deal, Grampa said. Before the end of the year the company, as he had predicted, went belly up, and Grampa lost all he had invested in it. No big deal — to Grampa financial gain was not important compared to doing what was right: it was simply a matter of principle. As my brothers and sisters and I learned growing up, to Grampa most things that people did in life were either a matter of principle or the lack thereof.

Whenever the opportunity arose, Grampa, like patriarchs of the past, imparted to his grandchildren bits of wisdom, such as, "No matter what you do in life, do your best, and always give your boss a honest day's work," and, "The only way to get ahead in the world is to be fair and honest in your dealings with others," and "In time, all liars and cheats are found out." But what was compelling were not the words, for we had heard it all before, in bits and pieces from school and church, mom and dad. What was compelling was the depth from which it came — his soul, his past. We knew it was true because he, as his father before him, had lived it out. It was a kind of historical and genetic "laying on of hands."

Grampa was raised to believe in democracy, capitalism, and that people of all races were created equal. He was a life-long Republican, believed in education, and voted for every school bond issue and tax increase. On the subject of religion, he once told me, as his father had told him, "It makes no difference if there's a heaven or hell, people should treat each other according to Christian principles. It's the only way to live." PRINCIPLES!

No question, about it Grampa was narrow-minded, set in his ways, always spoke his mind, feared no man, and, as one of my uncle's employees who knew him well once told me, "He would even argue with God." Once Grampa decided on a course of action, he was focused and committed to the end. He was a tough taskmaster but also had his gentle side. His family came first. He loved them deeply and had a heart of gold. He was one of the few men I knew at the time who wasn't ashamed to cry.

Grampa certainly had a zest for life and a good sense of humor. Occasionally, as we walked about his farm, he would break wind. At such times he would stop, cock his head, and grin. We always knew what was next: he would pause a moment, then speak. "Like my grandfather Drake used to say, it's always better to have an empty house than an angry tenant." In all my life, I have never met anyone quite like my Grampa Taylor.

My dad's temperament was more like his mother's. She was Frances Miller, and her family came to St. Louis by way of Toledo, Ohio. Her father Frank Miller was born in Bavaria, Germany, around 1844 and arrived in America in 1861. He settled in Toledo where he met and married Mary Wenz. Both of Mary's parents were born in Pfungstadt, Germany, near Darmstadt in the year 1819. They were part of the 48er's immigration that reached America in 1850.

Frank and Mary Miller had three children, Frances, George, and Albert. When Gramma's parents came to St. Louis I am not sure, but I do know when her dad died in 1913, her mother and 16-year-old brother Albert lived with her and Grampa. Her brother left a few years later, but her mother stayed until her death. I remember Dad telling me how much fun it was to have her as part of their family.

Both Grampa and Gramma were born the same year, only a day apart — Grampa on December 3, 1888, and Gramma the next day. Gramma spent her entire life in St. Louis. I remember her telling me how exciting it was as a young girl to attend the World's Fair; she would have been 15 going on 16 at the time. After graduating from high school, she worked at Southwestern Bell, where she became a supervisor. My grandfather met her at a Bell Telephone open house when he was still working at Laclede

Photos from top to bottom:

Top Left: Frances Miller Taylor.

Top Right: Roy Richie Taylor.

Center: Grandma and Grandpa Taylor, Aunt Dorothy and Dad.

Bottom: Dad, left, and Uncle Warren.

37

Gas. I remember him telling me how he was immediately taken with her. It was definitely love at first sight, and once Grandpa set his sights on something — well, you know!

I'm not sure what year they got married, but in due time she gave birth to three children. The first was Dorothy, who was born in 1912. My dad Harold was born in 1914, followed by his brother Warren a few years later. My Grandfather Taylor, like my Grandfather Henry Franke, also had his difficult times for not only did he lose his daughter Dorothy who died of diphtheria in 1925 at the age of 12, but just a few years prior to her death he lost both his brother Harold and sister Mabel to the great influenza epidemic that spread across Europe and America during the late teens.

I never got to know Gramma Taylor to the degree I did Grampa. To me she seemed strong and quiet in spirit and somewhat reserved. However, she had no trouble setting Grampa straight when he got carried away — "Now, Rich!" I can hear her say.

There wasn't much interaction between her and us kids. I know she played bridge, loved sports, and kept up with current events. It must have been from her as well my Uncle Harry that I inherited my love of history, for after her death we found numerous newspaper clippings that dealt with the history of this area.

GREENER PASTURES

In 1933 the Taylors moved across the River Des Peres into south St. Louis County where Grampa built a residence at 4100 Reavis Barracks Road, about a half mile east of Union Road. Dad had spent his freshman through junior years at Cleveland High School in the city. He would now spend his senior year attending Mehlville High School. At that time both St. John's Elementary School and the high school were housed in the same building. St. John's was a public not a parochial school located on the northwest corner of Lemay Ferry Road and Will Avenue, across the street from the present high school.

The original school was located at the corner of Green Park and Union Road and dates back to 1841. In the early days it was associated with St. John's Church although it was not a church school. In time its association was considered a conflict of the state - church doctrine of the State Constitution. Thus, around 1911, it was moved to Will Avenue on the Bollmann/Franke properties. In 1922 a new brick structure was built, and in 1925 the high school was added. My mother was the first and only member of her family to graduate from Mehlville High School. My uncle Louie Franke became a member of the Mehlville Board of Education, where he served for thirty-eight consecutive years.

Dad was one of the first "city boys" — maybe the first — to attend the high school. The other young men gave him a rough time, and it took a few good fights before he was accepted. It was there that Dad met Mom who at the time was in her junior year. After graduation, Dad spent a semester at the University of Missouri at Rolla. I'm not sure why he dropped out. One thing I do know is that he wrote Mom lots of letters. She had a box or two full of them upstairs in the attic, but about the time I learned to read, they disappeared. Someone once told me, and it might have been Dad, that he dropped out of college to help clear the land on the new farm Grampa had bought.

After the Great Depression, Grampa had decided to invest his money in land. So when he heard that the old Von Versen property was for sale he jumped on it. For years the property had been used as a pig farm. For some reason it had been taken over by the government and was to be auctioned off on the courthouse steps. On that day Grampa was one of the first ones there and was also the highest bidder.

The parcel was about thirty acres along the creek, just downstream from my mother's family, north of the intersection of Green Park and Reavis Barracks Road. Eventually Grampa sold his home up the street and, using the same blueprints, built anew. He also won points with the neighbors when he evicted the pigs. Dad helped clear the bottoms and went to work with Grampa in the foundry. Grampa also had two barns built so that it could be turned into a real working farm. Following high school, my Uncle Warren took up gardening. The newly cleared lands first grew field corn and later soy beans, and some of the best sweet corn ever grown in the county was raised there. The secret ingredient — pig manure!

Later Grampa added more land, which he would use as pasture, for the outrageous price of $200 an acre. Local folks talked about "that crazy old man Taylor." But, I can remember him telling me when I was just a lad, "Land is the only thing that keeps its value."

In 1937 Mom and Dad married and bought an acre of ground from Grampa directly across the street from his first home. Grampa had only one stipulation, that the house be built at least a hundred feet back from the road, for he knew that someday the road would be widened. Using Grampa's original plans, they built a nearly identical all-brick two-bedroom Tudor-style house — total cost of construction a little over $3,000.

In 1941, my mother's sister Mildred married Erwin Struessel, and they bought the adjoining lot next to my parents from my grandfather, with the same stipulation. As long as I can remember, Uncle Erv worked for the American Can Company. They had three children, Judy who was my age, then Gary and David.

My Uncle Warren married Anita Hoppe, who lived on Weber Road, which ran along the south side of the River Des Peres. Her dad William was the last milkmen in the area to deliver milk by horse. Aunt Anita and my mom both worked in my Aunt Mildred's beauty shop in Lemay up until the time they both married.

Uncle Warren and Aunt Anita lived with Grampa and Gramma Taylor for several years before building their own home on the west edge of Grampa's property. They had two boys, my cousin Bill, three years younger than I, and his brother Jack born several years later. It was shortly after their marriage that Uncle Warren took up dairy farming.

GRAMPA'S SCREENED-IN PORCH

As for our family, Mom said she always wanted to have ten children. She settled for six, all about two and a half years apart: my brother Harold, called Bob, followed by myself, Dorothy, Leonard, Joann, and Patsy.

Because both of my mother's parents died when Bob and I were very young, we spent most of our time with the Taylor side of the family. Grampa's farm and the creek bottom drew us kids like a magnet. Over the years, in addition to a working farm Grampa converted that old pig farm into a haven for wildlife. He built a spring house over one of the many springs that bubbled up all over the property. Eventually, five spring-fed ponds were built, and in time there were five-pound bass, channel catfish, and plump bluegill to be caught.

I can remember Grampa sitting on his boat dock, in his straw hat and khaki shirt and pants. He would pound a board on the dock, and the surface of the pond would boil with fish as he threw them tray after tray of day-old bread bought from a local bakery for two cents a loaf.

Some of my fondest memories are of my brothers and sisters, myself, and sometimes our cousin Bill sitting around Grampa on his screened-in porch. As you already know, Grampa came from a long line of hunters and fishermen, and while the bullfrogs boomed and the cicadas sang, he told old, very old hunting and fishing stories. These were the same kinds of stories that had been told over time, over and over again, with each generation clothing them in new times and new flesh. Somehow, the retelling made them all the better. Over the millenniums, from campfires to potbellied stove to screened-in porch, they had become — well, like a few other things that had been passed down, almost genetic.

And did Grampa have some stories! One of our favorites was about what happened after Great-grandfather Zachary got to the frontier town of Marion, Kansas. If you remember, he had gone there in search of prairie chickens. He had been told that when he got to town to look up a Mr. Drake, a well-known hunter and pioneer scout. Not only did he look up Mr. Drake, but after shooting forty-nine prairie chickens without a miss, he set his sights on Mr. Drake's daughter Edith, twenty years his junior.

40

"To make a long story short," as Grampa liked to say, "that's how I got my start."

They were married in 1885, and settled in Marion where they raised their four children Richie, Harold, Mabel, and Helen. There Zachary worked in the office of Case & Son Insurance Agency. It is said that he became a devout Christian, joined the Methodist Church, and became a lay minister. Of course, he continued to hunt and fish, but thereafter, never on Sunday. He preached weekly in the county jail and eventually had two chapels built in Korea, one each in memory of his wife and his daughter Mabel. I remember Grampa telling me how on numerous occasions his dad would quietly go into the local market, send the kids off, and then have the clerk make up a basket of food to be sent to some needy family. If there were children, he made sure some candy was included. When the clerk asked from whom he should say it was being sent, he would always say, "A friend." Zachary died in 1939 just a few months shy of his 92nd birthday.

Like his father and his Grandfather Drake, Grampa grew up to become a crack shot. After he moved to St. Louis, he gained the reputation of being one of the best quail hunters in the area, and hunters even came from neighboring states to match their hunting skills against his. One of the stories he enjoyed telling was about one of his old hunting partners, Denver Wright. Denver was a locally well-known millionaire and big game hunter. Grampa would laugh when he told us that Denver was such a poor shot that he had to take up hunting elephants because "he couldn't hit a broad side of a barn." We loved to hear how Denver once released a lion on an island in the middle of the Mississippi near St. Louis and had a lion hunt.

Photos from top to bottom:

Top Left: Roger, left, and brother Bob.

Top Right: Home — 4101 Reavis Barracks Rd., circa 1940.

Bottom Left: Grampa Taylor and cousin Bill — May 1956.

Bottom Right: Grampa's place.

THE OLD BRIER PATCH

To me, Grampa's place was paradise. Today I refer to it as the old brier patch. As my limbs lengthened and my curiosity increased, the brier patch grew along with me. Throughout most of the year, my home base was Grampa's and a few neighboring farms. The Missouri Pacific Railroad tracks paralleled the creek throughout most of its course and was my main access to different points of interest along the creek. In the fall and winter months, my territory often extended upstream as far as the old cement plant, west of Union Road, just a few bends southeast of Grant's Farm. On rarer occasions, it reached downstream all the way to where the creek bottom came to an abrupt end where the mouth of Gravois Creek enters the River Des Peres.

In time I learned that just below the junction of these two streams was once located Father Marquette's Mission of the Immaculate Conception, the first Euro-American settlement in the whole state of Missouri. I can't tell you how exciting the revelation was. It deepened my perception of time and place and strengthened my personal relationship with the land.

Beyond, on the north bank of the Des Peres, was the edge of the city. There stood the Monsanto chemical factory that rose like a white chunk of the Great Wall of China. Daily it belched up puffy white clouds of pollutants. From its base, gray ribbons of concrete flowed into the mystical city — St. Louis.

I remember several occasions in the late forties when Mom took me and my brother Bob by streetcar into the very bowels of the city, where our senses where flooded with strange new sights, smells, and sounds. It was all very exciting. Yet, it was always a relief to once again cross the Des Peres and return to the bottoms and the green fields. Yes, for us, the big city was a nice place to visit, but not to stay.

Author's field notes, February 18, 1957.

43

* * *

GREEN FIELDS AND WILD THINGS
or
UNIVERSAL EDUCATION

I can't spell
I can't punctuate
Guess that makes me
Un-ed-u-cat-ed!

But I can think
And I can feel
Golly gee —
That almost makes me real.

I was never very good in school
Not at all like most of yous.
Wouldn't dot my "I's"
Or cross my "T's"
Dreamin' about green fields and wild things.

But I could sing in the earth's tune.
Learned when and where the dogwood bloomed.
Know the creek's each bend and every verse
Back when Grampa's place was the center of the universe.

* * *

While I was growing up, nature, birds in particular, became a passion for me, so much so that I spent most of my free time in the creek bottom and most of my time in school daydreaming about the green fields and wild things. I was so preoccupied with nature that I missed a lot of the basics, such as reading and writing. Each year I drifted further and further behind the rest of the class. By sixth grade, I was already two or more years behind in grammar. Not only that, but I was lefthanded, right-brained, and stuttered. I eventually got over the stuttering.

Then, during the winter of that school year, the best worst thing happened: I contracted rheumatic fever. I was out of school the rest of the year and was tutored by the school principal, Ed Merryman, who later became Superintendent of Schools. Although I didn't quite catch up with the rest of the class, I did make it to the next grade.

My years spent in the creek bottom taught me things that weren't being learned in books, such as the powers of observation, reflection, seeing the interconnectedness of nature, an inter-unity and peace one finds in solitude. There also was this sense of being a part of the landscape — a belonging.

One spring day during one of my many sojourns I discovered that an old dead tree, used as a nesting site for many generations by several species of woodpeckers, had been blown down by a recent storm. This was a great disappointment. I hated to see the old apartment complex go to waste, so I cut out a section of what was once a flicker's nest. When I got it home, I made another cut a few inches below the entrance so that the top could be removed for cleaning. I then fixed the two pieces back together with wooden pegs and placed it atop a stump in our yard. By the end of the day, a pair of bluebirds had set up housekeeping. This was a rare treat, for seldom had bluebirds ventured into our neighborhood.

At one time, bluebirds in and around urban areas were not uncommon, but by the 1950's, the immigrant house sparrow, which was first introduced in Brooklyn, New York, in 1850, and the starling, introduced in New York City's Central Park forty years later, had taken over that niche. Thus, I felt privileged to have such a hearty pair move in and stake their claim. For the next few seasons my family and I enjoyed their flash of colors and cheery tune.

BLUEBIRDS AND HOLLOWS IN OLD, OLD TREES

The bluebird of happiness flew into my life one day
He flew in on a balmy springtime breeze
And he landed near a hollow in an old, old tree
And he sang a song so cheerfully.

Then he cocked his head and he must have said
"This is a good place to build a nest and raise a family."
So he found a mate and there he staked a claim
to all the land surrounding the hollow in the old, old tree.

And in that tiny hollow they laid soft brown grass
And feathers from the bluebird's breast
And there she lay four cloud-colored eggs
Time capsules of a bluebird quartet.

And through the summer they raised their brood
Chasing butterflies and baby bumblebees
And every time I heard their cheery tune
It made my heart lighter by a pound or two.

But then one frosty day the bluebirds flew away
And the hollow was cold and gray
But as the snow flew somehow I knew
That in the spring the bluebirds would be back again.

Then the snow did melt
And a balmy breeze I felt
Then I heard a warbling tune not far away.

The bluebird of happiness was back in my life again
He was flashing his red, white, and blue.
And it made me feel mighty thankful to Ma Nature who gave
The bluebird such a lovely tune.

Thank God for the bluebird and hollows in old, old trees.

* * *

46

5 - The City Starts Heading Toward the County

Following World War II, superhighways were built from the cities into the countryside. The Cold War was heating up, and these new highways were a part of our national defense plan to quickly move people out of urban areas in case of attack by the Russians. That's right — in case of an air raid, we were going to head south down those superhighways to places like Meramec Caverns and Fisher's Cave where we would hole up until the clouds of radiation passed over. Places such as these were being stockpiled with food and medical supplies.

Some families even began building their own bomb shelters. But then the media began asking the question. "What would you do if your neighbor wanted to stay in your shelter and there wasn't enough room, food, and supplies?" Wow! It was the kind of question that in the 1950's Americans seldom discussed. Like the new medium, television, that had recently entered our homes, we were accustomed to seeing everything in black and white. We were only comfortable with yes or no, right or wrong, true or false, questions and answers; none of this A and B and sometime C stuff. So almost as soon as the question was asked, the discussion ended, and so did most of the talk about building bomb shelters.

Well, the Russians never came, but the urbanites did — on those wide new roads, they could now travel farther faster. Like others before them, but in much greater numbers, they were fleeing the city in search of greener pastures.

* * *

BORN IN THE COUNTY

I was born in the county just south of St. Louis, Mo.
And my daddy worked in the foundry,
So to the city each day he would go.

But my uncles and my Granddad
They lived off of the land.
They were farming in the creek bottom
Just trying to make a stand.

And that's where I was raised.
The city was just a maze,
A nice place to visit but not to stay.

The city was headin' towards the county
With the sound of diesels and a cloud of dust
And soon the green fields and the wild things
All make way for pro-gre-ess, pro-gre-ess.

Now my uncles and my Granddad
They are all gone
And so are the green fields
Where all the wild things were found.

The children like others someday I suspect
will search for greener pastures
Where there ain't no pro-gre-ess.

But I'll stay here in the county
Because my roots in green fields grow deep.
But new seeds won't take root
in concrete.

So it's good-bye blue skies, so long green fields
With a sound of diesels and a cloud of dust.
The city was headin' towards the county
All make way for progress — pro-gre-ess.

The city was headin' towards the county
With the sound of diesels and a cloud of dust
And soon the green fields and the wild things
All make way for pro-gre-ess — pro-gre-ess.

* * *

48

PARADISE LOST

When I reached age eleven, Grampa gave me, like my brother before me, and as his grandfather Drake had given him, a 20-gauge shotgun. Due to Grampa's planning, the fields were thick with rabbit and quail. But by the mid 1950's, subdivisions, shopping centers, and malls were moving our way, and while I was intrigued, I was entirely oblivious to the eventual demise of the brier patch.

For a long time I had been in a state of denial about the development of the area, but slowly, ever so slowly, reality began to set in. One day I was hunting rabbits in Grampa's bottoms with no success. Across the creek was a field owned by a neighboring farmer that might just hold a few bunnies. So I crossed the old sycamore that laid across the creek to the other side. As I broke through the tree line, to my surprise I faced a field denuded of all vegetation. The once-rich topsoil had been stripped down to the subsoil. There sprouting in the field were the skeletal outlines of several new homes framed in two-by-fours. I had just met my first subdivision, up close and personal.

I was immediately struck by the small size of the lots. Facing the two structures, I stretched my arms out in front of me so the tips of my index fingers visually touched each building...and experienced a power-surge of energy. It was totally overwhelming. No thoughts, no analysis, just pure energy. When I think back to that day now, I visualize a painting by Charles M. Russell that shows an Indian hiding behind a large rock as he watches a long wagon train of settlers pass by. What is most striking about the picture is that the Indian is leaning forward with a hand cupped across his mouth — the universal expression of dumbfoundedness. And that's the only word I can find to describe that encounter.

Later I thought back to the last time I had visited the area the previous fall and remembered being a little curious about the wooden stakes with red ribbons tied to them around the border of the field. After thinking a little harder, I remembered a sign along Reavis Barracks Road that said something like "For Sale — 10.2 acres," followed by a phone number. It had been there so long that in time it had become just another part of the landscape.

Yes, the building boom was on, and if you had only, say, 10.2 acres of land, you could make a lot more money by clearing it and converting your corn and bean crops to two-by-fours. It's easy to see why it wouldn't take much convincing to get a tired old farmer to do just that.

* * *

TEN POINT TWO

Chorus: Ten point two, we'll subdivide it for you.
If you develop the whole tract
you'll double your money back.
Ten point two and all you got to do is
invest right now in a bulldozer not a plow.

Now the sycamores and the oaks will have to go, good folks,
and the rabbits and the squirrels bid toodle-loo.
We're gonna take the green grass down to the subsoil but don't frown for
the green will be back with dollar signs.

Chorus . . .

Yes, this here old farm used to grow lots of beans and corn
but now it will be sproutin' two-by-fours.
But that's quite O.K. for it pays better than hay
and the dividends will keep rollin' right on through.

It's the last undeveloped tract on this side of the map
and the land values are going through the trees.
So we'll tear the great oaks down
and if you stake your grades right now—
soon you'll be livin' on Easy Street.

Chorus . . . *Yes, trade in your cows for a 'dozer*
right now.

* * *

A couple of years ago, I was taking a new route to work, and situated on the edge of a subdivision, where I'm sure a farm once stood, there was a street sign that said it all — "Easy Street."

As my uncle Warren would soon figure out, he was in the right place at exactly the right time. The dairy farm he operated on my grandfather's farm proved to be hard work with little financial reward. I can remember as a young boy being fascinated when the modern milking machines were first used, but even with the new equipment, the profits were limited. Along with World War II came labor shortages and higher wages, and my uncle found it difficult to find and keep workers. Gradually he decided to get out of the dairy business altogether.

The Ford tractor which he bought for gardening he began using on week-ends to dig basements for local developers. Eventually he sold his cows, bought a bulldozer, and went into the excavating business full time. When he first told Grampa what he was planning to do, Warren said Grampa "jumped so high his head almost hit the ceiling." But by the end of the first year when he showed him his profits, Warren said "a broad smile spread across the old man's face."

After my first encounter with a subdivision, I must have rationalized that this was happening on the other side of the creek, not on Grampa's property nor my uncle's lands upstream. But things kept happening.

Back then, December 1 was the first day of trapping season in Missouri. Every year since I was eight or nine, my brother Bob and I, and later our brother Leonard, like our uncles before us, looked forward to opening day. Our cousins Roy Prestrope and Dale Franke also trapped the bottoms. From the start we worked out a gentlemen's agreement. The dividing line between the two trapping territories was set where Green Park Road and Reavis Barracks Road crossed the Gravois Creek. Our cousins' trapping grounds would be upstream of that point, and ours would be downstream.

By this time my uncle had dug all five of Grampa's ponds. This greatly expanded the habitat available for muskrats, our main quarry. The lakes also provided an extra bonus. Because muskrats were notorious for springing leaks, Grampa gave us $1.00 for each muskrat we trapped out of the ponds. On the average we also received a buck for each pelt we sold, usually to the F. C. Taylor Fur Company downtown. At the time, Taylor was one of three remaining fur companies left in St. Louis. If I had to choose the most exciting day of the year, the day my brother and I and our cousins looked forward to each year, it was December 1.

It was just a few days before the start of trapping season, and my brother Bob and I were scouting out the creek. As we rounded the first bend, we began to notice the smell of raw sewage, and when we reached the downstream edge of the new development, there it was — a huge pipe spilling frothy green water. Raw sewage was being dumped into our

51

creek! It was an example of what today is referred to as non-source pollution. The creek ran green downstream from that point. From that season on, we confined most of our trapping to the woods, edges of the fields, and Grampa's ponds.

OUT OF SIGHT, OUT OF MIND

Had I known my American environmental history at the time, none of this would have come as a shock. Actually, it was an old American tradition to dump waste into rivers and streams. Yes, since day one, Mother Nature had been providing the complete facilities with running water to flush away the sins of mankind.

St. Louis, of course, was no exception. By the 1840's, St. Louis' population was nearing the 50,000 mark. However, no plans had been made for human waste disposal. Each private residence in the city had its own privy (outhouse). That concept worked fine on the farm, but not in densely populated areas. So St. Louis, like most of the eastern cities and towns, began to get a little ripe.

Eventually the city fathers called in Henry Kayser, the City Engineer, and directed him to come up with some kind of disposal system. He did: the solution was to dump the sewage in the natural limestone sinkholes and caves that dotted the city. It was simple and cheap — out of sight and out of mind.

But in time, the sinkholes became blocked with debris and began filling up. Then in June of 1848, the city was hit with 17 inches of rain, and the sewage bubbled up to form a huge lake of waste on the north side of the city. It was thereafter appropriately referred to as Kayser Lake. This condition helped to bring on the great cholera epidemic of 1849.

Between July 1 and July 10 of that year, there were an average of 100-200 deaths a day. By the time it ended, the 1849 epidemic took between 4,500 and 6,000 lives, about 10% of the city's population. In 1854, with 3,547 lives lost that year, the city gained the distinction of being the cholera capital of the nation.

Back in 1849 the St. Louis City Council authorized the construction of a trunk sewer to drain Kayser's Lake. The project, however, didn't begin until 1850. Samuel R. Curtis, who was appointed the new City Engineer, was largely responsible for the completion of the project in 1851. In that same year, in his report to the mayor, Curtis proudly referred to the Mississippi as the "Great Trunk Sewer" of the St. Louis system. So it was, and so it remains.

Few Missourians know anything about Samuel Curtis the City Engineer, but if you're a Civil War buff you know Major General Samuel Ryan Curtis — the same man! Curtis was not only an engineer but a West Point graduate, and was serving as congressman from Iowa when the Civil

War broke out. In January of 1862, he was placed in charge of 12,000 troops stationed at Rolla. On the 26th of the month, Curtis advanced on General Price who was in command of the Missouri State Guard and supported Claiborne Jackson, the secessionist governor. Price had moved into Springfield after having defeated the Union troops under General Lyon in the bloody battle of Wilson's Creek. Lyon had been killed in the battle, and the rebels were preparing to take the state.

Upon Curtis's advance, Price withdrew from Springfield and across the border into northwest Arkansas. There he received reinforcements from General Earl Van Dorn, who was in charge of Confederate troops west of the Mississippi. Van Dorn added troops under General Benjamin McCulloch and Albert Pike who showed up with 2,000 Cherokee, Creek, and Choctaw Indians from the Oklahoma Territory. In all, they had a combined force of 25,000 men, greatly outnumbering Curtis's troops.

The showdown came March 7 and 8 at Elk Horn Tavern near Pea Ridge, Arkansas. Curtis's superior generalship forced a Confederate retreat. That battle, perhaps more than any other action, kept Missouri in the Union for the duration of the war.

In September, General Curtis was promoted to be commander of the new Department of Missouri, which in addition to Missouri included Kansas and Arkansas as well as the Indian Territory. Headquarters was in St. Louis. However, questions of abuse of power and mismanagement led to his dismissal in March of the following year. So Curtis's claim to fame in Missouri history is two-fold — he helped rid the city of cholera and the state of confederate troops. So much for Samuel Curtis.

Long after the construction of our first trunk sewers, the idea of dumping raw sewage into our rivers and streams continued not only in St. Louis but throughout the nation. By 1900, the historic River Des Peres was infamous, for it had become nothing more than an open sewer. Even to this day it is referred to by locals as The River Des Pew, River Des Stink, or River Despair.

Because the River Des Peres runs through Forest Park, it was temporarily boarded over so that its filth and odor wouldn't be offensive to fair-goers at the 1904 World's Fair. It wasn't until the depression years, however that the River Des Peres project was completed. The Gravois Creek, which flowed into the Des Peres, had no such system.

By the 1950's, the Gravois Creek and River Des Peres together were considered among the most polluted streams in the nation. Thus, in 1954 the Metropolitan Sewer District of St. Louis (MSD) was created through voter approval to clean up the mess in both the city and county. I remember how excited my grandfather was about the issue. He encouraged every one to vote for it and told me how it would bring the crawfish back to the creek. And it did. It also helped that in 1956, for the first time, the federal government began providing funding for construction of municipal

Major General Samuel Ryan Curtis.
St. Louis Mercantile Library.

sewage treatment plants. While MSD has done a commendable job, still today, as in the past, much of the St. Louis area sewage still goes untreated into the Mississippi — the "Great Trunk Sewer."

The above story can be told in a simple song. Here's all you need to know about the history of the St. Louis sewage system:

* * *

STINKY DINKY DOO

In eight-eight-eighteen hundred and forty-forty-two
St. Louis had nearly 50,000 people, but, boy, was it pee-yoo!
For it didn't have a sewage system even third rate
And that's why the city stank!

Chorus: *For it was stinky, stinky, stinky, stinky*
stinky, dinky-doo
And it was smelly, smelly, smelly, smelly
smelly pee-yoo!
St. Louie, Louie, Louie, Louie
What you gonna do
About your stink, a'dink, a'-dink, a'-dinky-doo?

Along came Henry Kayser, our City Engineer.
He said looky, looky, looky, looky
Looky listen here!
I'll take all that sewage and pump her in the ground.
We'll dump it in the sinkholes and the caverns all around.
And there'll be no more stinky, stinky, stinky, stinky
stinky, dinky-doo
There'll be no smelly, smelly, smelly, smelly
smelly pee-yoo.

Out of sight and out of mind, everything was fine
Until the summer of 1849.
In eight-eight-eighteen hundred and forty-forty-nine
It rained for nearly forty-forty-days and forty nights.
Seventeen inches of rain in June fell upon the land
And the sewage bubbled, bubbled up and ruined old Henry's plan.
Cholera and dysentery spread across the land
and the people held and thumbed their noses
At old Henry's plan.

Chorus:

Now along came Samuel Curtis,
Our new City Engineer.
He said looky, looky, looky, looky, looky and listen here
I'll drain that Kayser Lake, we'll tunnel beneath the town,
We'll plug it in the Mississippi,
No more reason to frown.

But now the Mississippi River was —
Chorus:

The bullfrogs and the catfish they all began to croak.
They didn't think a whole lot of Mr. Curtis's practical joke.
Now over a hundred years have passed
And the river flows on by,
But now we got MSD and things are lookin' fine
Because they're cleaning up the —

Chorus:

* * *

THE FINAL DAYS OF THE BRIER PATCH

In 1958, between my junior and senior year in high school, Grampa finally sold twenty acres of his bottomland along with what we called the island lake, not to developers but to the owners of Channel 4 TV station. The purpose was to build a 1,200-plus-foot transmitting tower and control station there. These took up very little land, less than an acre, but a much larger plot of land was needed around it to secure their guide lines. There weren't many sites left in the area suitable for such an operation, so Grampa worked himself a sweetheart of a deal. Under the contract it was agreed that for the rest of his and Gramma's life, they would have full use and control of the land. That meant he could continue to farm the bottom land or even lease it. Grampa would also have full use and control of the lake, and even the new owners would have to ask permission to fish in it. By this time in life, Grampa's arthritis was making it difficult for him to get around. He had given up hunting but continued to fish, so to cap off the deal, the new owners agreed to build him a paved road to the lake. Grampa was still one shrewd businessman.

By that time, Grampa really was "Old Man Taylor." His fingers were as gnarled as the limbs of an old, old tree, and his limp was so bad that he walked with a cane. His days were numbered, and he knew it. It was time to seriously think about his family and cashing in his chips. The Missouri Pacific Railroad ran right down the middle of Grampa's property, paralleling the creek as it did through the Franke properties. He had his land re-zoned for light industrial use and eventually it sold for many times what he had paid for it. So much for "Crazy Old Man Taylor."

Within a few years of the Channel 4 deal Grampa decided to sell all of his property, his home included, to his two sons for but a token of its value. This was before the $600,000 inheritance tax exemption was passed. Of course, it was agreed that Gramma and Grampa would live in their home for the rest of their life.

In the winter of 1960, I had left home to attend Southeast Missouri

56

State College in Cape Girardeau. By the time I graduated in the summer of 1964, an era, a way of life, was all but over. Gramma died first in 1960, Grampa in 1968, and Dad in 1971, and I watched as pieces of my paradise were sold off in bits and pieces. Eventually my uncle moved his office from one of the old dairy barns to Grampa's residence.

It's something of an irony that the same equipment used to dig grandfather's ponds later were used to fill them in to make way for my uncle's expanding business and other development. I never felt any animosity towards my uncle, my own father, or even the developers, for I know they were living out the American Dream. At that time in history, the slogan most everybody believed in was "All make way for progress." What I did feel with the combined passing of each family member and each parcel of land was a deep since of personal loss — I was losing my most valuable "belongings."

Over the years, I often questioned how Grampa could have allowed the land to be sold off in bits and pieces. But in time I have come to realize that the creek bottom was my homeland, my brier patch, not Grampa's. His was the Flint Hills of Kansas and the Cottonwood River that ran through it.

To him that old pig farm that he converted into a silk purse was but a bit of fresh air, a way of keeping in touch with his roots, his contact with the earth and universe. But to him it wasn't sacred ground. Mostly he viewed it as an long-term investment to be bequeath to his sons and their families. It was all part of Grampa's values, his PRINCIPLES! But, having just said that, I can't help but think back to his words: "Land is the only thing that keeps its value."

Cottonwood River catfish — Grampa Taylor, center; brother Harold, right; unknown individual, left.

Today, all but one of Grandpa's spring-fed ponds — the lake with the island — are bulldozed over or filled in. The Franke properties upstream are even less recognizable. The only natural area that remains today is the creek and the narrow green strip that runs along it — the last remaining lifeline of the wild things. Thank God for floodplains.

Uncle Oscar was the first to sell out when he retired from farming in the early 1960's, but he continued to be active in antiques for some time. Harry finally sold out to the developers and bought a newer, more productive farm in Columbia, Illinois, which he worked with his son Marvin. That had to have been around 1963. While I'm not sure of the year, I clearly remember the last time I saw his place above the Gravois Creek, the house my mother was born in.

I was home from college one weekend, and developers had already been grading the land. It was only a matter of time before they would be razing the old farm house. When I got home, Mom told me that she had heard that kids had broken into the house and demolished it. She asked if I wanted to go with her and take a look at it. It was already evening and we wanted to get over there before dark.

As we drove up to the frame structure, we weren't prepared for the emotional shock that greeted us. The front door to the screened-in porch, as well as the entrance door, had been ripped off their hinges. All the windows had been broken out, and glass littered the floors along with plaster from the ceilings and walls. We hardly recognized the floor plan. This was the house that all of Mom's brothers and sisters had been raised in. As we walked about, she keep repeating something like, "Well, it was going to be bulldozed down in a few days." But even though we knew that, it was as if that home, that family, and all that living and the memories that went with it had been assaulted and trashed.

Soon it was getting dark — time to leave. As we passed through the living room area and headed towards the door, Mom paused and looked down at her feet. There smashed on the floor was the mantel that once hung above their fireplace. She stood there staring at it a while, her arms folded and pressed tight against her breast, as if to contain her feeling. Whereas before her voice and words were solemn and measured, it now quavered. "That was our mantel where we hung our stockings each Christmas."

We stepped out into the night, and few words were spoken on the way home. Reality had finally slapped me upside the head. On that dark night it was clear that an era had finally ended, and that there was no way to turn around and go back. It was one of life's toughest lessons.

Grampa Franke on screened-in porch, holding Mom.
L–R: Aunt Mamie, Aunt Mill, Aunt Florence, Aunt Lillie, Aunt Irene.

Brothers-in-law who married Henry Franke's daughters, 1940.
L–R: Harold Taylor (Agnes), Fred "Fritz" Perstrope (Ella), Herman
Muelker (Irene), Erwin Wuch (Florence), Charles Von Tagle (Mamie),
Erwin Struessel (Mildred), not shown Clarence "Hats" Emie (Lillie).

PART III

BEYOND
THE BRIER PATCH

After entering high school, my horizons began to expand beyond the creek bottom. I can remember becoming good friends with George Moore, the old naturalist at Rockwoods Reservation. It was he who introduced me to the Missouri Audubon Society and the Webster Groves Nature Study Society. I also remember spending my sixteenth birthday working at Lake of the Ozarks State Park. The following fall, I worked part-time at a Mom-and-Pop grocery store on the southwest corner of Lindbergh and Lemay Ferry Road. With my dad's encouragement, I bought a used canoe and began exploring our state's rivers and streams. Dad thought I was working and saving my money to buy a car, but that was the best worst misconception Dad ever made about my life. What I really wanted was a good pair of binoculars. Buying that canoe had a most profound effect in my life.

Later, I went to college, got my degree, and started teaching. My dream was to teach in my home district, as my older brother Bob did. But that was not to be; I ended up teaching at Hoech Jr. High in the Ritenour School District in the St. Ann and Overland area. I married and had two sons, Steve and Ken, and lived in St. Charles for a few years. It was a nice town, but like Overland and St. Ann, it wasn't home. By the time I returned to South St. Louis County, I had become a stranger in my own homeland. Not only were the green fields and wild things gone, so was most of the glue that once bonded family, clan, and community together. Brothers and sisters, aunts, uncles, and cousins, had been flushed and scattered like a covey of quail, and having lost our home territory we found it difficult to regroup.

Thus, more lost "belongings" — not only land, but home, family ties, clan, community. As I mentioned in *Watershed–1*, "community" today is but intersecting lines on the compass.

61

6 - The Great Awakening

About the time I started teaching, the ecology movement was beginning to take hold. Around 1963, I remember seeing a wall plaque belonging to a salesman that proudly expressed the view that the world was an unfinished product and that God had given man the tools and mind to make this a better place to live. That view was not something to be questioned. I can remember an old General Electric commercial done by Ronald Reagan that always ended with the phrase, "Progress is our most important product." But even before the 1960's, in my mind, Herbert Spencer's doctrine that "Progress . . . is not an accident, it is a necessity . . . it is part of nature," was ripe for debate. I wrote the following parody as a personal response to that plaque.

* * *

GREED

Greed, greed, greed, the American creed
A Bill of Rights to fulfill all our needs.
Born inside of us is a tiny seed
An instinct which is known as greed.
And God gave to us an unfinished earth
and the human mind so that we could convert
The trees, the trees, to two-by-fours,
Streams, streams, streams to reservoirs.

Consume, consume, consume, develop, invest —
These are the things we love the best
They have replaced Mom and apple pie
As the values that we hold most high.

Extinct, deplete, and domesticate
All go to prove we are the superior race.
Ecology, Conservationist —
Communist ploys to arrest our progress.

So give me, give me, give me all that I can own.
Money, money, money — how we love it so.
And our children must do their very best
To exceed our own greediness.

* * *

If we had to pick one single event that got the country as a whole to start the questioning process — to reevaluate the progress-at-any-cost doctrine — it was the publication of the book *Silent Spring* by Rachel Carson in 1962. The book dealt with the dangers of pesticides, not only for wildlife but for humans. Other studies and works followed, showing similar dangers related to air and water pollution. It was then that people finally realized that their own health was at risk, and increasing numbers began demanding that the government take action.

It should be made clear at this point that our country's concern for the welfare of our environment didn't begin in 1962. Americans had already established an impressive track record. For example, in 1872 Congress set aside Yellowstone as the world's first national park. Yosemite became our second national park in 1890, and by 1916 the number had reached 13. In 1875, George Perkins Marsh founded the American Forestry Association, which in 1889 helped to push a bill through Congress empowering the President to establish national forest lands. By 1907, Presidents Harrison, Cleveland, and Roosevelt had set aside 59 million acres of forests.

In 1886, George Bird Grinnell founded the first Audubon Society, which eventually created some of the country's first wildlife sanctuaries and worked for federal laws protecting non-game birds. In the early 1900's, the American Bison Society was also formed to save the last few free-roaming buffalo. On the home front, in 1936 the citizens of the state of Missouri, through the initiative process, established the Missouri Conservation Commission (today the Department of Conservation).

What makes 1962 special is that before that date, individuals and their representative organizations were primarily concerned about the preservation of natural areas and wildlife. Collectively they were referred to as preservationist and/or conservationist. After 1962, there was first a gradual and then a rapid shift of emphasis towards the protection of our own species. In short, individuals and organizations began looking to the federal and state governments to protect us from the by-products of our own civilization.

Works such as *Silent Spring* also pointed out the interconnectedness of all living things. Instead of just focusing on individual species, we began thinking in terms of ecosystems. These individuals and organizations now working to preserve the environment were referred to as environmentalists and/or ecologists. They seriously began questioning business as usual and the premise that progress is impossible without pollution.

The movement gradually picked up steam with the passage of tough federal and state clean air and water quality laws in the 1960's. A high-water mark was reached in 1970 with two major events: the nation's first Earth Day celebration and the passage of the National Environmental Protection Act (NEPA).

Wisconsin's U. S. Senator Gaylord Nelson is credited with spearheading the nationwide celebration that on April 22, 1970, brought together over 20 million Americans. The effect was to make it clear to national and state governments that there was a broad-based environmental movement afoot, and it looked like it was here to stay. Washington and Jeff City lobbyists, move over!

While the Earth Day celebration was still in its planning stages, the huge Santa Barbara oil spill occurred off the coast of California. Shortly thereafter, U. S. Senator Henry Jackson introduced the Environmental Protection Act, which was passed before the end of the legislative year. That act led to the creation of the Environmental Protection Agency and the requirement that all new projects involving federal lands or federal money could not be approved until an environmental impact statement was filed. Overlooked at the time by Congress was that these studies were also subjected to public review and comment. Soon environmental organizations were employing not only lobbyists but lawyers.

As 1970's advanced, Congress passed, with the blessing of the Nixon administration, the Endangered Species Act and stronger clean air and clean water legislation. The provisions of these acts had to be included in the filing of future environmental impact statements. All the above added to the environmentalists' clout.

Soon the states, through either new federal mandates or their own initiatives, began following suit. In 1974, the Missouri General Assembly consolidated most all of the state's departments and agencies, outside the Department of Conservation, that deal with the environment and placed them under the Department of Natural Resources. Today the Missouri State Division of Environmental Quality is responsible for carrying out both state and federal regulations.

In 1976, Missouri citizens approved another initiative petition, this one establishing a 1/8 cent sales tax for conservation. Then in 1984 they approved an additional 1/10 cent sales tax to be used for soil conservation and state parks. When it comes to matters pertaining to the environment, Missouri has rightfully earned the title of the "We'll Show Ya" state.

THE COUNTERREVOLUTION

The cost of protecting and cleaning up the environment is high, and it cannot be measured in dollars and cents alone. Jobs were being lost, and it didn't take long for a counterrevolution to start building.

I remember General Motors saying that it would be too costly to meet the new federal air quality standards and Ralph Nader taking them to task. Along the banks of the River Des Peres, the National Lead Company was shut down in the early 1970's, and the ecologists were blamed. Many industries were convinced, right or wrong, that progress and pollution went hand in hand and that you "can't have one without the other."

* * *

PROGRESS AND POLLUTION
(to the tune of "Love and Marriage")

Progress and pollution, progress and pollution
Go together like insane and institution.
This I tell you, brother—
You can't have one without the other.

Try , try, try, to separate them—
It's an illusion.
Try, try, try, and you will only come up with
Too costly a solution.

Progress and pollution, progress and pollution
One of America's finest institutions.
Keep the smokestacks toiling
So we can have full employing.

Now don't worry, don't worry
About a little bit of dirt in the air.
For just a dollar, a surgical mask
Nicely you can wear.

Progress and pollution, progress and pollution,
Hats off, salute it — progress and pollution.
Keep the smokestacks toiling
So we can have full employing.

Now don't worry, don't worry
About emphysema and hepatitis
For it's industry's contribution
Towards zero population.

Remember! Congress was told by General Motors
"There ain't no way
That is, it just don't pay—
You can't have one
Without the other."

* * *

65

SMOKE GETS IN YOUR EYES

There's a lot of negative things we've done to our air, waters, and the earth in general. Today two of the most hotly contested issues being debated are the greenhouse effect and ozone depletion.

It didn't take St. Louis long to become aware of the damaging effects of acid rain on manmade structures and plant life. As early as 1906, two years after the World's Fair, it was noted by the local newspapers that air pollution was killing trees in Forest Park, and by the 1820's nurseries were refusing to sell evergreens to city residents. The Missouri Botanical Garden was even considering a move, and in 1925 they acquired the 1,600 acre Arboretum at Gray's Summit, 30 miles southwest of the city.

By the mid-1920's, St. Louis had earned the reputation as the dirtiest town in the Mississippi River Valley. Anti-smoke ordinances had been passed as early as the 1890's, and in 1923 the St. Louis Chamber of Commerce established a committee on smoke abatement to educate the public and industry on proper stoking of furnaces. In 1924, a Smoke Regulation Commission was created with the power to license and inspect new furnaces. All of the above measures, however, failed to clear the air. In 1926, the Citizens' Smoke Abatement League estimated that smoke was costing St. Louisans about 15 million dollars a year. They also noted that the United States Department of Health estimated that the annual soot deposit in the city was 870 tons per square mile, three times that of Pittsburgh. Things continued to go downhill, and on the following Christmas, the smoke was so bad, it was dubbed the "Black Christmas of 1927."

The main problem was that from the very beginning, St. Louis had been acquiring their coal from across the river in Illinois. It was soft, and it was very dirty — on the average 30 percent ash and 6 percent sulfur. But more important, it was very accessible and cheap, and by the 1930's St. Louis was burning 4,000,000 tons of it a year. Things only got worst after the Depression. Businesses began stoking up again, and the increased number of automobiles on the roads added insult to injury.

By then, what became known as the "midnight noons" were a common occurrence, particularly during the fall and winter months. On such days the smog was so bad that motorists had to turn their headlights on in the middle of the day. A retired businessman friend of mine recently told me that on one of those days, he had to drive around the 3100 block of Easton Avenue (now Martin Luther King Drive) three or four times before he could find his office.

Finally, in 1934, the city mayor, Bernard Dickman, asked Washington University for help. The University pointed them towards Raymond R. Tucker, who taught mechanical engineering. Tucker was a local boy, a graduate of St. Louis University High School and Washington University

School of Engineering. Following graduation, he taught at the university until 1923. In that year he gave up teaching and moved to Tulsa where he worked in the oil industry. In 1927 he returned to the university as an associate professor.

Upon the mayor's request, the school gave Tucker release time to try and solve the city's air pollution problems. Mayor Dickman directed him to study the situation and then report back to him.

In that study, Tucker recommended that all coal should be washed before firing. After being reviewed by a citizens' committee, the recommendation was enacted into law in 1937. Tucker was appointed as the new Smoke Commissioner and was empowered to seal furnaces of the most serious offenders. In an attempt to block the ordinance, the soft coal industry took the city into federal court, but the ordinance was upheld.

However, the ordinance had little visible effect on the air quality of St. Louis. Things came to a head in the winter of 1939, when in November there were three solid weeks of dense smog. The worst day of all was on the 28th, thereafter referred to as Black Tuesday. By then it was clear to both Tucker and the mayor that the only way to clear the air was to totally ban Illinois soft coal. Time to bite the bullet.

On December 11, 1939, following Tucker's official recommendation, the mayor appointed a Citizens' Smoke Elimination Committee, which endorsed the proposal on February 24, 1940. Immediately, the opposition's propaganda machine went to work maintaining that such an ordinance would be too costly and would particularly place an unfair burden on the poor. A bill was introduced to the Board of Alderman, and the mayor had to use all his political muscle to prevent the bill from being weakened by amendments. In April of 1940, the ordinance was passed.

The problem was where St. Louis would get enough clean coal, for they figured there would be at least a million-ton-shortfall. The answer was Arkansas anthracite. The city learned that the per-ton cost was comparable to Illinois soft coal, but shipping made it considerable more expensive. Eventually the Fresco Railroad agreed to lower their rates by 30 percent, which was later matched by the Missouri Pacific. Consumers were now able to get their coal at a reasonable cost. Almost immediately the air began to clear. The following winter, the skies were generally smog-free, and businesses began scrubbing their buildings down, giving them fresh faces.

Along with the new ordinance, other factors began falling into place. The railroads agreed to switch to diesel power, and the Mississippi Valley Fuel Company Pipeline had just been extended to St. Louis. Thereafter, Laclede Gas did a booming business in installing inexpensive new gas furnaces.

If awards were ever given for environmental success stories in St. Louis, this one would most likely take first place. In fact, the St. Louis

Post-Dispatch received a first place Pulitzer Prize for its coverage of the story, and Raymond R. Tucker not only became a recognized expert on smoke abatement but went on to serve as mayor of St. Louis for twelve consecutive years (1953—1965). He won his first two elections by the largest majority ever in the city's history.

Throughout the country, the switch was on. More and more home-owners and industries were converting to oil and natural gas. With the landmark passage of the Clean Air Act in 1965, the federal and state governments began setting stiff air quality standards. It looked as if it was only a matter of time before coal would be phased out. However, by the mid-1970's, Old King Coal would one again be rising from the ground. In the meantime, the country had a love affair with the atom.

Raymond R. Tucker (seated center) meets with coal dealers and city officials on April 23, 1940 to discuss importing Arkansas coal to be sold to consumers for $5.50 a ton.
St. Louis Globe-Democrat photo — St. Louis Mercantile Library.

ATOMS FOR PEACE

By 1940 our country was seriously seeking and implementing alternative energy sources such as natural gas, but in 1941 the United States entered World War II, and by the war's end in 1945, the new buzz word was "atomic energy." Though the war had ended, the Cold War was just heating up. Thus, our government continued to develop more complex and destructive nuclear weapons, while at the same time promoting the "Atoms For Peace" idea. The latter made for good PR; after all, Americans believed that something good must always come out of something bad. Thus, the new energy switch naturally swung towards nuclear energy.

Americans were sold on nuclear power because they were told how cheap it would be to produce huge amounts of energy with just a little bit of uranium. What the government didn't tell the public — perhaps because in their initial enthusiasm they hadn't even bothered to think about it — was that we didn't know what we were going to do with all the waste and the unknown costs of creating nuclear power. In hindsight, it seems inconceivable that our country would have undertaken the production of the most dangerous energy source known if we had been aware that there was no safe way to dispose of its waste. The attitude was, we'll cross that bridge when we get to it. Let's get started.

St. Louisans would learn all about this waste problem the hard way. In 1989, area residents first became aware that there was an estimated 2.3 million cubic yards of waste scattered throughout the metropolitan area. They also learned that the federal government estimated the cost of removing it at close to a billion dollars. How did we get ourselves in such a predicament?

It all started in April of 1942, when Arthur Holly Compton, a former professor of physics at Washington University, met with his old friend Edward H. Mallinckrodt, Jr., of Mallinckrodt Chemical Works. Compton had come from the University of Chicago where he was involved in the government's secret project to develop the "ultimate weapon," the atomic bomb. The word was that Hitler was also working on such a weapon, and it was believed that he was several years ahead of the United States.

Compton wanted a commitment from Mallinckrodt to the federal government to purify the four tons of uranium needed to build the first atomic bomb. Because of its highly volatile nature during the purification process, no chemical plant he had talked to was willing to take on the project. Mallinckrodt believed that by using the right amount of ether to cool the liquid uranium, they could prevent an explosion. The agreement was signed with a handshake. Fifty days later, after Mallinckrodt had completed a successful experiment, they were off and running.

On December 2, 1942, the uranium processed here in St. Louis was used in the University of Chicago experiment that proved that it was indeed possible to build the atomic bomb. It was also the cyclotron at Washington University in St. Louis that produced the plutonium used to trigger that first bomb. However, it wasn't until August 8, 1945, the day after President Truman gave the order to drop the bomb on Hiroshima, that the Mallinckrodt employees learned the importance of their work.

During the Cold War, Mallinckrodt continued to purify uranium at its downtown plant for the federal government's nuclear weapons production. They built the country's first commercial uranium-fuel production plant in 1956 at Hematite, Missouri, 35 miles south of St. Louis. The following year they started up operations at Weldon Spring in St. Charles County on land acquired from the the the U. S. Army by the Atomic Energy Commission. The land had been part of the Weldon Spring Ordnance Works which between 1941 and 1945 produced dinitrotoluene and trinitrotoluene (DNT and TNT) for the Allied Forces during World War II. In all, the Atomic Energy Commission built 44 buildings on the 205-acre site. Taylor Excavating (my uncle's business) even provided a number of cranes and operators used to build the plant.

It was the first automated operation of its kind, and its original goal was to produce 5,000 tons of uranium a year while at the same time providing maximum safety. Between 1957 and 1966, the plant was actually cranking out an average of 16,000 tons a year. During these peak years, Mallinckrodt employed over 1,000 workers in its uranium division. Then, as suddenly as it had begun, so did it end. In 1966, the Atomic Energy Commission decided to consolidate all its uranium feed production at the National Lead Company plant in Fernald, Ohio, and the Weldon Spring site was placed on standby status. It was never reopened.

In 1968, the Army conducted a crude cleanup. The purpose was to clear the site so that the government could begin making Agent Orange there. In the process they dumped 900 truckloads of contaminated material into a quarry four miles to the southwest of the plant. There it joined waste from TNT and DNT that had been produced at Weldon Spring during the war years. The Army also sent 81 railroad carloads and 7 truckloads of contaminated equipment to Knoxville, Tennessee, to be decontaminated. However, shortly thereafter the Agent Orange project was canceled.

In 1985, the U.S. Department of Energy was assigned the task cleaning up the entire mess. They soon found out just how crude the previous cleanup was when they discovered a ton of thorium in one building and 100 pounds of pure uranium metal scattered about the grounds. They estimated that the cleanup would take twelve years to complete at a projected cost of $400 million.

In addition to Weldon Spring, there are other sites in the St. Louis area that need to be dealt with. These include portions of the Mallinckrodt plant in North St. Louis, the Airport Storage site, and the nearby Latty Avenue storage site in Hazelwood. The areas surrounding these last two sites have also been contaminated by runoff, leaching, etc. And, there's the West Lake landfill in Bridgeton, Coldwater Creek, haul roads, and other properties.

Interestingly, there were at least four other sites that the government had lost track of and might not have ever been discovered if it weren't for some detective work on the part of local anti-nuclear activist Kay Drey and the St. Louis Post-Dispatch. These include the Dow Chemical Company plant in Madison, Illinois; the General Casting Plant in Granite City; the Small Arms Plant in North St. Louis; and the Tyson Valley Powder Plant, now the Washington University Tyson Research Center directly across the river from where I live. The good news is that all the above were temporary storage sites and primarily needed to be checked out to see how much, if any, radioactive residue remained.

What is to be done with the 3.2 million cubic yards of remaining radioactive waste? That was the $700 million question. Nationally, it's a $320 billion question. The federal government has clearly stated that there's not enough money or human resources to complete the job, and with the balance-the-budget, cut-spending, end-federal-mandate mood of the American people and Congress, it looks like soon there'll be even less.

At present, the Energy Department has no intentions of dealing with the waste buried at the Hematite site in Jefferson County nor the West Lake landfill in St. Louis County. Hematite comes under the authority of the Nuclear Regulatory Commission, and neither it nor the Energy Department claims responsibility for West Lake. As for the remaining sites, the original plan was to consolidate all the radioactive material in St. Louis and St. Louis County and cap it at a new location in the area. But neither the city or county governments nor local environmental organizations were in favor of such a plan. They all want it removed to a non-urban site.

Kay Drey suggests that it be stored within a 6,500-acre tract next to the Callaway County Nuclear Plant site along with the power plant's own waste. Union Electric, which owns the plant and the land, doesn't like the idea. So, for now, we're at an impasse.

The Weldon Spring site is a different situation. There the government already owns the property and is planning to consolidate the waste in a 45- to 58-acre area and enclose it in a rock-capped bunker. That means removing over 10,000 truckloads of debris from the contaminated chemical plant and the quarry southwest of the plant.

The Energy Department is well aware that such a bunker is a short-term response good for perhaps only a couple hundred years. But some of the uranium to be stored there has a half-life of 4.5 billion years. That means that in 4.5 billion years, the radioactivity will have been reduced by one half, and in another 4.5 billion years by another one-half, etc. In addition they need to clean the contaminated lakes in the Weldon Spring Wildlife Area, which pose a danger to St. Charles' well water system.

The Callaway County nuclear power plant near Fulton and research reactors at the University of Missouri campuses in Columbia and Rolla are the state's other nuclear plants. Back in 1973, Union Electric announced its plans to construct two reactors at the Callaway site at an estimated cost of just under one-half billion dollars. The first reactor went on-line in 1984 and cost $3.1 billion. Due to a statewide vote and overestimated energy needs, the second reactor was canceled. The Callaway reactor is licensed for an initial 40 years, though it will probably not last that long. Important questions remain about decommissioning and dismantling the plant: how much will it cost? can the huge, contaminated building be dismantled? where will all the waste be stored? It has been estimated that it will cost about the same amount to raze it as it did to build.

At present the Federal Government is studying the possibility of building a national repository for high-level nuclear waste at Yucca Mountain, Nevada, at a projected cost of $8.3 billion. The repository, which was planned to be completed and receiving spent fuel by 1998, is still on hold. To date Union Electric has paid over $74 million into the Department of Energy's repository account with no guarantee that it will ever be built or opened. The government is now looking at the year 2010. By that date over 50,000 metric tons of nuclear fuel waste will have accumulated across the country.

Scientists within and outside of the Department of Energy are debating whether Yucca Mountain is as safe a place to build the repository as they once believed; questions include geological and earthquake hazards. They plan to do more testing of the area into 1998 and then decide. The citizens of Nevada have already decided they don't want it. So it looks like another classic stand-off.

It's obvious that the American fascination with nuclear power has soured. Not only are people becoming shocked by the problems of removal and storage of its waste and the high cost associated with it, they are increasingly concerned about the safety of these plants — as well they should be. The eye-opener was the Three Mile Island accident which began on the morning of March 28, 1979. Government authorities say that the reactor came within thirty minutes of meltdown before it was brought under control. Though no one was killed then, or sixteen months later when a controlled purge of the reactor building was carried out, 220,000 people had to be evacuated on several occasions. The total cost of the accident has been estimated at $2 billion dollars, not including health costs to workers and the public.

Then there's the tragic Chernobyl incident in the Soviet Union in 1986, which to date is officially responsible for at least 400 deaths, unnumbered medical problems, and environmental contamination which spread beyond the Soviet Union into Scandinavia, Britain, Southern Germany, and Greece. The estimated cost in dollars thus far: $12 billion. Recently several Russian scientists have been speaking out and saying that the damage was much greater than originally reported. Not only that, but some scientists warn that the reactor is continuing to leak and that the other reactors operating in the area are also unsafe.

There is also concern about the increasing number of nuclear plant shut-downs occurring each year in our own country. According to government safety reports, there were 16 between May and June of 1976, 44 between August and December of 1982, and as many as 195 between May and September of 1984. Although some did contaminate workers, most of these incidents did not release radioactivity into the environment in levels that exceed federal permissible standards. Many of the problems were found to be due to human error, defectively designed and fabricated parts, or a combination of the two. Just last year (1994), the government reported 299 environmental safety and health problems at 13 U. S. nuclear weapons facilities containing plutonium.

The last nuclear power plant order in our country that was not subsequently canceled was placed in October, 1973, and 114 nuclear plants once on the drawing board have been canceled. Also, due to high maintenance and repair costs, 16 have closed before their 40-year license expired. It has been projected that this number will eventually include 25 percent of the 109 plants presently in operation. No question about it: nuclear power has fizzled and is in a rapid state of free fall.

As I wrote this section, I thought back to an event that occurred in 1960. Following my high school graduation, I worked at Barnes Hospital in the mail room until entering college in January the following year. In addition to sorting the mail, I also delivered it to all the departments in the entire Barnes complex and was called upon by the admitting office to take patients to their rooms. One day I took a distinguished-looking gentleman and his wife to his room. I remember it seemed strange that his room already had several flower arrangements when we arrived. As I turned and prepared to leave, his wife smiled and handed me a silver dollar. Not only was it strange to receive a silver dollar, but I think it was the only time I was tipped. When I got back to the mail room, one of the older employees excitedly asked, "Do you know who you just took up there?" I just shook my head and showed him the silver dollar. He told me that it was Dr. So and So — "You know, one of the guys who worked on the atomic bomb." I'm not sure, but I think he might have said Dr. Compton. As I think back, he sure resembled Dr. Compton's photograph. I don't remember what ever became of that coin, but I'll never forget Dr. Compton's role as a major figure in the environmental history of St. Louis.

7 - The Energy Crisis

Even though for decades we were expanding our nuclear facilities, it wasn't fast enough to meet our ever-growing energy needs, and disturbingly, we and the rest the industrial world became increasingly dependent on foreign oil. For a number of reasons, U. S. oil producers had been investing more and more of their capital into Middle East production. It was cheaper to extract oil and ship it here than it was to produce it domestically, which, of course, translated into greater profits. Greed again.

In time, the Middle East countries felt they were being taken advantage of. In 1960 they formed the Organization of Petroleum Exporting Countries (OPEC) which in 1973 pulled off its first oil embargo. Immediately, oil prices shot up, and it wasn't long before our country found itself in double-digit inflation and growing trade deficits. Long lines began forming at gas stations, and states began rationing fuel supplies. In 1974, the Federal government mandated that the states lower speed limits to 55 mph or risk losing federal highway funds. In 1975, the federal government passed the Energy Conservation Policy Act, which also required states to implement a number of energy conservation programs. Included in these were the promotion of car pooling and public transportation as well as a right-turn-on-red policy.

In Missouri, the Fuel Allocation Program under the Public Service Commission was created to determine fuel priorities. In 1975, it was renamed the Missouri Energy Agency and became part of the newly created Department of Natural Resources. It was the agency's job to move a step beyond allocation and come up with recommendations for laws, programs, procedures, and policies for state and local governments to ensure wise and efficient use of energy resources. In 1977, the Missouri Energy Agency became the Missouri Energy Program and was given the added responsibility to work closely with the U. S. Department of Energy. Its scope continued to expand, and in 1979, when the second oil embargo hit, it became the Division of Energy, and so it has remained.

It was during that second embargo that the federal government instituted price controls, including a price ceiling on oil, which remained until 1981. In 1987, the Feds allowed the speed limits to be bumped up to 65 mph outside the metropolitan areas, and at this time there's a bill in Congress to do away with federal speed limits altogether.

While most economists today agree that price controls was a bad move, and even helped to create the problem, it did produce an unexpected windfall for energy conservation. The U. S. Energy Department took Exxon Oil Company to court for over-pricing. Exxon was ordered to place $895 million into a Petroleum Violation Escrow account. The money from the fund was to be distributed between the states and territories, to be used to make restitution to consumers. In 1986, the fund had grown to $2.1 billion, and Missouri received $42 million, which it used as seed money to start up a number of state energy programs.

As part of the price control program, the Congress had also set different price ceilings for oil removed from old and new wells. Companies were allowed to charge higher prices for oil taken from the newer wells. Some companies began using a steam process to remove oil from old wells and then sold it at the new oil price. They too were taken to court, and their fines were placed in the Stripper Well Program, which like the Exxon account was distributed to the states.

With these moneys, the State Division of Energy has done a commendable job in working with state institutions, private business, and the general public to conserve energy, and has also provided limited funding for the development of new energy sources. In spite of this, there remains a huge supply and demand gap between our state's and the country's demands for energy. To date, we are still dependent on foreign oil, fossil fuels, and nuclear energy.

In fact, the energy crisis created a temporary revival of the waning coal industry. From the start of the crisis, the industry was quick to remind us that coal was our most abundant source of energy, with enough to last for over a thousand years. So, in our panic, there was a movement to relax air-quality standards and promote a return to coal. We also began looking at other fossil fuels as a source of domestic energy. Soon federal and state grants were directed towards such projects as coal gasification, and western congressmen insisted that the development of oil shale was another great idea. None of these have proved to be a viable solution. But throughout much of the energy crisis, Old King Coal was again dustin' off his robe and fittin' on a crown.

* * *

OLD KING COAL

Old King Coal was a merry old soul
And a merry old soul was he.
He fueled American industry for over a century.
But Old King Coal was a dirty old man
So we began to put him to rest.
But since the energy crisis
He's a-being resurrect.

75

Old King Coal he's a-stirring around,
He's a-rising from the ground,
He's dustin' off his robe, he's a-fittin' on a crown.
He's sittin' on a golden throne with smokestacks in the back,
He's a huffin' and a puffin,' everything just turnin' black.

Since the energy crisis, we really been in a stew,
The Congress and the President don't quite know what to do.
And with the winter coming, they don't want to be left in the cold
So they turn to a false idol, which is known as Old King Coal.

He called for his pipes
He called for his stacks
He called for his fiddlers three.
Now their fiddling up the country with pollution
Can't you see?

Black clouds are rolling
Emphysema on the rise
Don't go out in the rain
You'll get acid in your eyes.

If we only listened thirty - forty years ago
And let the sunshine in
We might have saved our soul.
But instead of looking to the sun
And seeing the light
We turned towards coal
And darkness of the night.

For Old King Coal was a merry old soul
And a merry old soul was he
He fueled American industry for over a century.

But Old King Coal was a dirty old man
So we began to put him to rest.
But since the energy crisis
He's a-being resurrect.

Old King Coal is still a dirty old man.

* * *

SEEING THE LIGHT

It had always seemed logical to me that the most ideal source of energy would be the most direct one, the source of all energy on earth — the SUN. The supply is unlimited, direct, nonpolluting. So why haven't we directed as much money and research on it as we have, say, nuclear energy?

For one thing, the sun is a hard thing to monopolize. In other words, it would be very difficult for the oil industry and the utility companies to control its development and marketing. Thus, lobbyists representing the above groups and legislatures with vested political interest in them worked hard to keep government funding for solar research at a bare minimum. So most of the advancements in solar energy have come from the private sector.

In 1956, Bell Laboratories premiered the world's first photovoltaic power plant. It was made up of dozens of wafer-thin solar cells wired together on a 8-square-foot panel. By the 1960's, this new power system was efficient enough to power satellites. By 1973, solar energy cost was still 50 times more expensive than conventional electricity. However, because there were no moving parts, units were almost totally maintenance-free and were ideal for use in isolated areas void of other energy sources. So by the 1980's, solar energy was finding wider and wider commercial and domestic use.

Solar energy is ideal for supplying heat at or below the boiling point, which is used for heating homes and cooking, accounting for 30-50 percent of the energy used in industrial countries and an even greater amount in least developed countries.

Because of its ease of adaptation, energy-poor Third World nations were the first to embrace the new technology on a wide scale. Already in India there are over 6,000 villages that now use solar power as their main energy source, and the concept has spread to Sri Lanka and Indonesia.

By the 1980's, solar electricity found increased use in our own country due to cost reductions of over 70 percent. Already there are over 1 million active solar heating systems and 250 thousand passive solar homes in our country. Passive solar homes are positioned and built to take advantage of the sun's direction at different seasons as well as the natural flow of warm and cool air.

By the 1990's solar energy was making real inroads into urban areas. Such systems can be used to help upgrade existing power sources by reducing the costly expansion of power plants and utility lines. Also, advances made by the electric vehicle industry will soon be applied to home and industrial use, thus providing cheaper storage systems. In some parts of our country, solar energy has already reached parity with more traditional sources. It is believed that by the end of this decade solar energy cost will be as low as 10 cents per kilowatt-hour and may drop as low as 4 cents shortly thereafter. And just think, all this progress, at minimum expense to taxpayers.

* * *

THE HOLE

My socks got a hole in it.
Darn it —
Thank you, Momma!

My bicycle tire got a flat.
Patch it —
Thank you, Daddy!

My soul got a hole in it.
Fix it —
Thank you, doctor!

Thank you, thank you, thank you,
One and all.

Oh, look up there,
The sky's got a hole in it —
See it!

Look, it's getting bigger and bigger —
Over there!

Oh, it's getting hotter and hotter —
Feel it !

Fix it, fix it, fix it,
Somebody fix it please! !

* * *

Before leaving this section we need to put to rest controversies over the hole in the ozone and the greenhouse effect. First of all, there are two kinds of ozone, the good kind and the bad kind. The good kind lies far out in the stratosphere where it helps to filter out a large portion of dangerous ultraviolet rays, which in high concentrations increases skin cancer among humans and stunts photosynthesis in plants. In fact, ultraviolet radiation is one of the main reasons life evolved in oceans. Without the ozone layer, neither plant or animal could have survived on earth. It was the gaseous waste emitted by bacteria and other one-cell organisms that helped to produce the protective shield that allowed life forms to first come ashore as well as providing the oxygen we and other animals breathe.

The bad ozone is the low-lying kind made up of high concentrations of carbon dioxide. While this type of ozone, like the other, occurs naturally, since World War II the amount of carbon dioxide in the atmosphere has more than doubled. Carbon dioxide released from factories mixes with other pollutants to create a dangerous chemical stew known as smog. To be specific, smog forms when hydrocarbons along with nitrogen oxides react together in the presence of sunlight to form ground-level ozone or smog.

Because this type of ozone is found at low altitudes, it also traps ultraviolet rays close to the earth, thus increasing the earth's temperature. This is what scientists call the greenhouse effect. The increased burning of the rain forests also increases carbon dioxide and low atmospheric ozone build-up.

Scientists began checking the stratospheric ozone levels in Antarctica as far back as 1956. It wasn't until 1975, however, that they noticed the first small hole. Thereafter, particularly since 1987, the hole has grown alarmingly. In 1974, atmospheric chemist Dr. Sherwood Rowland and his colleague Dr. Mario Molina, both from of University California, Irvine, discovered that ozone depletion is caused by chlorofluorocarbons (CFC's). The main culprit is freon, once used as a propellant in hairspray and paint and still used in refrigeration and solvents.

CFC's were developed about 60 years ago as a substitute for chemicals that were considered harmful to humans. Because of the stability of their molecules, they were considered nontoxic when they came in contact with humans. The problem is that this stability allows them to enter the ozone layer intact until they are split apart by the ultraviolet rays entering the stratosphere. This action releases the chlorine atoms that eats away at the ozone layer. It has been estimated that in the last forty years, the amount of chlorine in the atmosphere has increased by 600 percent, thus the concern about increased ultraviolet radiation and the negative affects associated with it.

A new theory now being expounded says that ozone depletion is primarily caused by volcanic activity, not synthetic chemicals. This theory maintains that as long as there have been volcanic eruptions, there have been major fluctuations in the ozone, so, not to worry. How this erroneous theory came about, and how volcanoes cannot be responsible for the hole in the ozone is explained by Sherwood Rowland in the June 11, 1993, issue of *Science* magazine. While it is true that volcanoes emit hydrogen chloride, when they erupt they also release huge amounts of water vapor which dissolves most of the hydrogen chloride on contact. Thus, most of the chlorine never reaches the stratosphere because it is washed out in the rain. Rowland maintains that measurements following the massive eruptions of El Chichon in 1982 and Pinatubo in 1991 showed that only small amounts of chlorine were added to the ozone layer. So, how to account for this new theory?

In 1976, following the eruption of Mount Augustine in Alaska, a geologist compared the levels of chlorine found in ash from the volcano with glassy lumps of magma believed to have also been expelled in the eruption. In 1980 he wrote a paper stating that the magma had twice the levels of chlorine as did the ash. Thus, he hypothesized that huge amounts of chlorine must have been released into the stratosphere — his estimate was 100,000 tons. Applying the same theory, he then calculated the amount of chlorine that would have been emitted by a much larger volcano that erupted in California some 700,000 years ago. That amount was 289 million tons, 570 times the amount of CFC's produced in the entire world in 1975! But this theory didn't take into account the above-mentioned effects of water vapor on chlorine.

Though the theory was dismissed by atmospheric chemists, that didn't stop the ozone doubters from making the most of it. Eventually the theory was printed as fact in several books as well as The Wall Street Journal and several other newspapers. But it was Rush Limbaugh's 1992 bestseller *The Way Things Ought To Be* that drew its widest audience. To Limbaugh, it was just another example of environmentalist wackos at work.

But so much for speculation. On December 19, 1994, Anne Douglass, Deputy Project Scientist of NASA's Upper Atmosphere Research Satellite program, announced that there was now conclusive evidence that the annual ozone hole over the South Pole was caused by manmade CFC's. On September 15, 1991, NASA launched its upper-atmosphere research satellite from the space shuttle Discovery. The satellite's instruments measured stratospheric temperatures, winds, and trace gases that react to ozone. From these data, NASA have concluded that approximately five-sixths of the ozone-destroying chlorine in the stratosphere comes from CFC's. What they found was the presence of fluorine in amounts that correspond to chlorine in the stratosphere. Fluorine is the "fluoro" part of the chlorofluorocarbon molecule. NASA pointed out that there is no natural source of fluorine.

In spite of this compelling evidence, some folks still can't see the hole through all the smog, and if you can't see it there's no need to fix it! So — "keep the smokestacks toiling so we can have full employing."

8 - A Niche in Time

In time, the creek bottom was but a memory, and by the 1970's, most of South County was fully developed. What had happened there was also occurring in east and north parts of the county. Because of its rugged terrain, large portions of West County would become the developer's last frontier. There, a major barrier to total development are the existing greenways — scattered pockets of state and county park lands, along with Rockwoods Reservation and the Meramec River floodplain. In these areas, the bulk of the county's wild things, and myself, are making our last stand.

For all but a few years of my life, I have lived in St. Louis County, and as I said in my song, my roots had grown deep here. In 1978, in search of greener pastures, I discovered Castlewood, a small town at the west end of the county.

Before the development of superhighways and Lake of the Ozarks, the village of Castlewood and the Meramec River served as a major weekend retreat for a large number of St. Louisans. Many arrived in Castlewood by train from stations in St. Louis and Kirkwood. There were boathouses for canoes and several hotels. Club houses dotted the hillsides. During the summer months, as many as 10,000 people could be found on Lincoln Beach.

Just down the hill from me used to be the "Lone Wolf," one of the oldest country-western bars in the St. Louis area. Like the town of Castlewood, it has a long and colorful history. The place was built by Eddie Paul, who owned a large chain of dry cleaners in the St. Louis area. He was so anti-union that he became known as the "lone wolf", and that's how his establishment got its name. During the 1940's and 1950's, the place was notorious for its gambling and "pitching whiskey." In short, like the rest of Castlewood, was a hangover from the speakeasy era. In those days Castlewood was indeed the country, and so was its music. And so it has remained long after the passing of Eddie Paul. The "Lone Wolf" eventually closed and was bought by Wildlife Rescue which rehabilitates and relocates area wildlife which have become victims of urbanization.

Today I live at "Nuthatch," a little niche between the bluffs overlooking Castlewood State Park and Tyson Research Center, which today houses both the Wild Canid Center and the World Bird Sanctuary. Also, to the east and west, respectively, are Lone Elk and West Tyson County Parks. Below me flows the Meramec River, the umbilical cord that connects my being to the earth and universe. On most days and on moonlit floats I usually have the river to myself. At night I can hear the barred owls, the coyotes, and the wolves from the Canid Center. It all produces such a lovely illusion, for just a few miles away are the busy communities of Ballwin, Manchester, and Ellisville. I seem to have the best of two worlds.

* * *

LIVING AT THE END OF TOWN ON THE EDGE OF TIME

I live at the end of town
Sittin' on the edge of time.
High on an Ozark bluff
Everything's just fine.

In the village of Castlewood
Everything's just as it should.
I'm happy I'm livin' at the end of town
On the edge of time.

And the river flows gently by
As it has for all of time
And those cottonwoods and sycamores grow free
And the summer's usually mild
And at night the coyotes howl
And the Lone Wolf's down at the bottom of the hill.

But every Monday to Friday, you know
Towards the city I got to go
To earn my share of nickels and dimes.
But after I head on home
And reach the valley below
I'm happy I'm livin' at the end of town
On the edge of time.

I'm happy I'm livin' at the end of town
On the edge of time.

* * *

82

PART IV

REALITY CHECK

'We have found the enemy and they are us.'
—Pogo

You can run and you can try to hide, but the ills of mankind will eventually find you. Then all you can do is move on, or dig in and make your stand.

When I first moved to Castlewood, it was some time before I had any trash pick-up. So every week or so, I would haul my trash to the West County landfill just off Big Bend and Sulfur Spring Road, directly across from the northeast border of Castlewood State Park. The West County landfill began operations in the early 1970's, and by the time I moved to Castlewood it was already a massive operation. Over the years, I watched as whole hillsides were stripped down to bury the treasures that used to be. In time a mountain of alternating layers of refuse and fill rose above the Meramec River. As one now canoes down the river and rounds the bend towards the park's boat ramp, the landfill's bald knob dominates the scene. Each time I see or smell it, I wonder how long it will take before we, as a country, really get serious about recycling our solid waste.

West County landfill, as viewed from Castlewood State Park.

9 - Buried Treasures

Under state law, the Missouri Department of Natural Resources (DNR) is charged with the responsibility of issuing landfill permits for up to 15 years and is also charged with monitoring them. While on a county level, the Planning Commission is empowered to grant conditional use permits (C.U.P.), the County Council retains review authority over the Planning Commission and can conduct its own review of the C.U.P. prior to the permit becoming effective. In other words, they have the final say.

The Department of Community Health and Medical Care (DOCHMC) is the County counterpart of the DNR. Under the St. Louis County government 1987 Waste Management Code, they are responsible for issuing annual operating permits and monitoring all aspects of construction and operation of county landfills.

It should be noted that St. Louis County, in addition to handling most of its own waste, also receives most of the waste from St. Charles County and the City of St. Louis. However, a portion of St. Louis County waste also goes to Illinois landfills. A good question might be, if the County is responsible for long-term planning, and providing waste disposal facilities in the County is such a major problem, why hasn't the County done more to encourage St. Charles County to handle more of its own waste? I don't know, but the County landfill operators must love the business. One thing for sure — landfills have become modern-day gold mines.

With the recent closing of the Maryland Heights site, there are but four sanitary landfills now operating in the County. Due to more stringent State engineering requirements and local opposition, the last permit applied for, in 1977, wasn't issued until 1986. In addition to sanitary landfills, there are also a number of demolition landfills in the County and one in the City of St. Louis that accept building material and non-household waste.

I talked to Joe Trinko at the DNR regional headquarters in St. Louis County concerning the status of landfills in the St. Louis area. He told me that the projected life expectancy of existing landfills in the St. Louis City and County is between 10 and 15 years, with his personal estimate being closer to 10 years. I also asked Steven Parker, an Environmental Specialist at the office, about long-term plans for dealing with solid waste. His response was, "Strange you should ask that question. Until recently, we had a statewide plan in operation, until the Cole County Circuit Court found part of it to be unconstitutional." Here's what happened.

In 1990, the Missouri General Assembly passed Senate Bill 530, which created the Omnibus Solid Waste Management Law. The purpose of the law was to help counties and municipalities to achieve a 40 percent reduction in solid waste by 1998. Under Senate Bill 530, the Missouri DNR was required to divide the state into solid waste management regions. St. Louis County, the City of St. Louis, and Jefferson County make up one of these regions. These regions were encouraged to form a solid waste management district. Each of these districts was required to develop a solid waste management plan. Among other things, the law required the plan to address the separation of household waste, procedures to minimize the introduction of small quantities of hazardous waste, and the establishment of educational programs. Any county or city with populations greater than 500 which chose not to join a district was still required to develop and implement its own plan by January 1995.

Unlike previous legislation, this bill required considerably more time and expense to prepare and implement. For example, the DNR manual alone was 300 pages. As a result, several cities and counties complained that the requirement to draft and implement such a plan was too costly and filed a lawsuit alleging that Section 230.325 of the law violated Article X Section 21 of the Missouri Constitution. That section requires the state government to appropriate and disburse funds to pay for increased cost of any new activity or service or an increase in the level of any activity or service beyond that required by existing law.

In October 1993, the Missouri Supreme Court ruled that if any part of Senate Bill 530 violated the above constitution guidelines then those portions of the bill would be unconstitutional. The court thus sent the case to Judge Byron L. Kinder of the Circuit Court of Cole County for review. On February 1, 1995, Judge Kinder found Section 260.325 of the bill unconstitutional and entered an order preventing the DNR from requiring solid waste management districts, as well as counties or cities which are not members of a district, to prepare and implement detailed solid waste management plans. Thus, since the above ruling, the DNR has stopped reviewing new plans. However, this ruling in no way prevents solid waste management districts, counties, and cities from preparing and voluntarily implementing new plans. It should also be noted that other sections of Senate Bill 530 are still enforceable.

As of January 1, 1991, the law banned the dumping of oil, batteries, appliances, and tires in sanitary landfills, and as of January 1, 1992, yard waste was also prohibited.

It should be noted, however, that banning the above items from sanitary landfills in no way eliminates the problem. A good example would be the 30-acre St. Louis composting facility now located in Peerless Park. In the last couple of years, there have been numerous complaints of foul odors emitting from the fermenting mass of yard waste. The mayor of Peerless Park complains that the DNR and county should monitor the operations more closely. Whatever, moving waste from one place to another is not the answer. Metro area residents can use only so much compost. In addition to recycling, perhaps we need to look at new uses for yard waste and other refuse, and perhaps direct more attention towards trash-to-energy conversion.

Because of growing concerns about such matters, in November 1991, county voters approved a 5 percent surcharge on the gate fee paid by haulers who dispose of trash in St. Louis County landfills. These proceeds are being used to fund a variety of countywide recycling programs.

The most recent good news, however, is that since the summer of 1994, the demand for recycled materials has been moving dramatically upward. The Kirkwood recycling center, the first in St. Louis County, set up some 25 years ago, paid $16 a ton in 1994 to have newsprint hauled off, but in March 1995 it was receiving $30 dollars a ton. A year ago they were getting $10 a ton for cardboard; now it's a whopping $140 a ton. During the same period, aluminum increased from 34 cents a pound to 55 cents, and glass has held steady at 17 cents a pound.

The demand for recycled newsprint has also increased worldwide. The Jefferson Smurfit Corporation, the world's largest paper recyclers, based in Clayton, Missouri, received $100 a ton for used newsprint delivered to East and West Coast docks during the summer of 1994, an increase of 40% from the previous spring. That trend has remained steady into 1995. Then there's the interesting story recently reported in the Post-Dispatch stating that Browning Ferris Industries, which operates several landfills in the metro area, received a call inquiring if the company had any landfills for sale. Why? To be mined for recyclable material. Interesting! "There's gold in them there hills."

But while we are seeing some real progress, the situation involving the West County landfill and Castlewood State Park continues to deteriorate. In September 1972, a County Council hearing was held on the request for an conditional use permit to allow the creation of a 128.9-acre sanitary and building material landfill located on the southeast corner of Sulfur Springs road in west St. Louis County. The Council approved the conditional use permit (C.U.P.) on November 21, 1973, and the landfill was licensed to operate until February 1981 based on a November 1973 start-up date, or until it reached a capacity of 4,000,000 cubic yards, whichever occurred first. The landfill, however, didn't begin operations until April 1974. Also, under the C.U.P., the fill was not to exceed the neighboring ridge line in height, which was between 616 to 620 feet mean sea level. C.U.P. permits were to be reviewed on a five-year basis.

In 1985, West County Disposal was granted a new C.U.P. that extended its use until June 30, 1990. Under the new permit, instead of reserving the southernmost 525 feet of the site for construction and building rubble, sanitary waste was now allowed to extend to all but the last hundred feet. This modification was conditioned on the provision of a protection levee being constructed along the south property limit. This condition was never met.

In June 1987, a St. Louis County Waste Management Code was adopted. In compliance with code requirements, West County Disposal submitted a permit modification report to DOCHMC in late 1989. The report requested, among other things, permission to increase their vertical elevations limit at the northern portion of the site. In view of the nearing expiration date, the Planning Commission voted to extend the existing C.U.P. for ninety days. Due to public concerns about extending the permit beyond the June 1990 expiration date, the Planning Commission elected to conduct an extensive review of the C.U.P. conditions governing the landfill, which was followed by a public hearing on October 29, 1990.

It should be noted that while the 1987 Waste Management Code exempts existing landfills from the application requirements, the County endeavors to update existing waste facilities with each permit renewal, and this was the first renewal subsequent to the 1987 code.

It is interesting to note that when considering positive reasons to extend the landfill, the Planning Commission noted that the southern portion of the site . . . "is uniquely 'buffered' from residential uses by Castlewood State Reservation [park] on the west, the Union Electric employee recreation area to the east, the filled portion of the landfill to the north, and the Meramec River and railroad right-of-way to the south." In other words, the Planning Commission views the Meramec River and Castlewood State Park as excellent buffers to the adjoining landfill. Does this suggest that new landfills should border other greenways such as Babler State Park and Rockwoods Reservation?

On the negative side was, among other things, "the alleged violations of the operating conditions by the current landfill operator." By 1990, the landfill, without County or State approval, had reached a height of 668 feet above sea level, 30 feet over the limit set by the County. And now the West County landfill operator James B. Becker was asking that they be allowed to expand the landfill south towards the Meramec River to its new height of 680 feet. As an end result, permits were granted by both the County Council and State DNR in spite of the fact that both the County and the DNR had evidence that the landfill was contaminating Castlewood State Park. Under the new C.U.P., the landfill has a projected life expectancy to June 21, 2001, or until it reaches 7.3 million cubic yards of fill.

* * *

THE WEST COUNTY DUMP

Every Friday it seems
I bury some dreams
High on a hill
In the West County Dump.

I just follow my nose
down the Sulfur Spring Road
to the gate
That takes me right into that dump.

I just enter on through
Pay my buck or two
And follow the truck in the lead.
At the end of the line
The 'dozers I find
Bury the treasures that used to be.

There's tattered old shoes
Empty bottles of booze
Old letters from Johnny to Jane
Broken dollies and lost wedding rings
And the memories that went with them.

There's rusty old cars
Washing machines galore
And worn out old pots and pans.
Gee, would it be neat if the trash at our feet
Like dreams could be recycled again.

We'll have full bottles of booze
Shiny new shoes
More letters from Johnny to Jane
Smiling dollies and bright wedding rings
And promises without an end.
And those rusty old cars would go once more
Now all shiny and bright
And just could it be we'll save energy
As we travel the new highways of life.

But as I leave the scene
I awake from my dream
And I'm struck by reality.
That for now it seems
I'll still buy my dreams
High on a hill in the West County.

* * *

PARK OR LANDFILL?

The landfill has now been fermenting for a number of decades, and methane gases have made their way to the surface. Though vents have recently been installed to burn off excess gases, on certain days when the ozone levels are high and the wind is just right, a stench fills the valley.

These gases have also worked their way though the layers of limestone and have popped up on the east edge of the park and, as of 1995, have killed over 600 trees. I predict that it's only a matter of time before methane will be entering the basements of surrounding new homes. It's quite possible that when that happens, some of the local residents will have to be evacuated, as has happened at several older sites in the metro area.

What is most disconcerting to me is that the DNR did not take aggressive action to stop the issuance of a new C.U.P. permit. It was clearly noted in the Planning Commission's permit review in 1990 that "Significant concern was raised in 1984-1985 by the Parks Division of the MDNR over the defoliation of park trees adjacent to the western perimeter of the landfill." Why then didn't the DNR take the appropriate action to deny the permit? And why did it take until March 18, 1991, for the DNR to ask the attorney general's office to take civil action against the landfill for repeatedly dumping trash 40 feet higher that permitted? In addition, they maintained that over the last five years, the landfill failed to maintain a buffer zone and had failed to control the releases of liquids and methane gas. They requested civil penalties of up to $1,000 a day for each day a violation occurred. The landfill's operator James B. Becker claims that the department was retaliating for a suit that he and other landfill operators filed in 1990 against one of the state's new recycling laws. In that case, the Cole County Circuit Judge James McHenry found in favor of the operators.

In 1992 the DNR released a major study on the health of our state parks. Their conclusion was that the major threat to the parks is encroachment from surrounding environs. This was particularly true of those in or near urban areas. Because of its location, Castlewood State Park was considered among the most threatened. The DNR suggested that a protective buffer zone be established around such sites, and since that report has purchased several huge tracts of land adjoining Johnson's Shut-ins and several other parks.

The only observable action taken by the park department at Castlewood State Park to date has been the relocation of a hiking trail away from the contaminated area. It's my understanding that recently an out of court settlement was agreed to whereby West County Disposal Ltd. would provide $54,000 in materials and services to the park.

In short, nothing tangible has occurred to stop the continual degradation of our park. It should be made clear that damage payment doesn't qualify as mitigation. In like situations, mitigation is often used to replace land lost with new land. As the landfills extend their operations into the next millennium we can only expect more encroachment and more financial restitution. The river, the park, the wild things, and Missourians deserve more than that.

At the present time the State Parks Department receives a cut from the 1/10 cent sales tax earmarked for state parks and soil conservation that was approved in 1984 and again in 1988 by Missouri voters. Unless renewed, the sales tax will run out in 1998. This year, a number of bills have already been introduced in the state legislature to extend the tax. Each has its own ideal as to how much the tax should be and who else should receive a piece of the pie. One bill would even merge the State Park Department with the Department of Conservation.

10 - Ignorance and Bliss

The problems associated with such operations as the West County landfill came as no great surprise, giving our history of solid waste disposal. Totally unexpected, however, was the discovery in 1983 that part of Castlewood was contaminated with dioxin. Our village would thus become one of 27 known dioxin-contaminated sites in eastern Missouri. Debate on how best to dispose of the contaminated waste has greatly strained the relations between a large number of county residents and their county government on one hand, and the DNR, the governor, and the Federal EPA on the other.

* * *

WAY DOWN UPON THE MERAMEC RIVER

Way down upon the Meramec River,
Times Beach, Mo.
That's where my heart is turning ever,
That where I lost my home.
All the world is sad and dreary
everywhere I roam.
Oh, floodwaters and dioxin
Takes me from my home sweet home.

* * *

It wasn't until near the end of the Vietnam war that the general public became aware of dioxin and its possible dangerous side effects. Some soldiers who had come in contact with the herbicide known as Agent Orange, which was used as an defoliant, were returned home with skin rashes, tumors, and an assortment of other complaints. Years of testing and debating followed before the government finally acknowledged a probable relationship between dioxin and two forms of cancers: non-Hodgkins lymphoma and soft-tissue sarcomas. In 1991, peripheral neuropathy, a nerve disorder, was added to the list.

Most Americans were never aware that our own U. S. Forest Service had also used Agent Orange in some of our National Forest lands such the Mark Twain National Forest right here in Missouri. For some years they experimented with defoliating large tracts of hardwoods and then seeding the area in pine. Many of the local ranchers picked up on this and began using the same method as a way to expand their range lands. So Agent Orange, like DDT and nuclear waste, become a domestic by-product of war.

On October 27, 1982, the Environmental Defense Fund in Washington released to the press a list of 14 confirmed and 41 other suspected dioxin sites in Missouri, and Missourians — St. Louisans in particular — received their crash course on dioxin. On November 10, 1982, government officials announced that the town of Times Beach was contaminated with dioxin.

Times Beach had an interesting beginning. Back in 1925, the St. Louis Star-Times, as a unique promotion technique, gave away a free Times Beach lot when individuals bought a $67.50 six-month subscription to their newspaper. Because of the popularity of the Meramec River as resort area at the time, the promotion was highly successful, and soon club houses filled up the 500-acre site. Over the years, most of them were converted into permanent residences, and by 1982 the town had a population of 2,242.

On November 30, 1982, the Environmental Protection Agency started taking soil samples at Times Beach. The following week the sampling was halted due to record flooding of the Meramec River. On December 23, because of fear that the floodwaters might increase the residents' risk of exposure, the Missouri Department of Health along with the U. S. Centers of Disease Control said that the town should be evacuated.

Why was dioxin considered such a dangerous chemical that an entire community had to be evacuated? First of all, dioxin is not just one chemical but a family of 75 chemicals. Though some forms of dioxin occur naturally, it is primarily a by-product of manufacturing created by burning chlorine-containing wastes. First discovered in the environment in measurable amounts in the 1920's, these toxic chemicals are dispersed mainly by wind and eventually find their way into lakes, rivers, and soil, and then work their way through the food chain. Chlordane, once the number one pesticide used for termite control, primarily enters our rivers and streams through leaching and run-off. Like DDT, it accumulates in fatty tissues. Since the 1980's, chlordane has been responsible for a number of fish advisories in the lower Meramec River as well as in sections of the Mississippi and Missouri Rivers. In 1988, chlordane was banned by the Federal government.

In St. Louis, Monsanto no longer manufactures chlorine but uses it in the production of a large number of products such as pesticides and plasticizers. In response to those who would like to ban all chlorine products, the chemical industry says that would be totally unrealistic. They claim that 35 percent of all the chlorine is used to produce other chemicals, and

14 percent alone is used in making pulp and bleaching paper.

After considering a number of options, and over the objections of many of the residents, the federal and state governments felt that evacuation from Times Beach should proceed. On February 22, 1983, both the federal and state governments announced that they had come up with $36 million from the Federal Emergency Management Agency (FEMA) for a Times Beach buy-out. In April 1985, the city was disincorporated, and in September of the following year the last family was relocated.

Some observers might conclude that the discovery of dioxin at Times Beach might have been the best worst thing that could have happened. Because the town had not complied with Federal floodplain requirements, it had been denied flood insurance. With the dioxin buy-out not only were residents paid for their homes but given money to relocate, and in time, millions were paid to them in lawsuits. However, for most residents, the health risk associated with dioxin contamination wasn't worth it. For a good percentage of the population, Times Beach was their home, and as in the past, they would have cleaned up, rebuilt, and stayed — dioxin or no dioxin. What some residents and environmentalists find interesting is that the state was apparently aware of the contamination as early as 1972.

OIL AND DIOXIN — BAD MIX

In May 1971, Russell Bliss, a St. Louis area waste hauler, sprayed an indoor horse arena in Lincoln County, Missouri, with waste oil laced with dioxin. Shenandoah Stables is located at Moscow Mills, the property of Frank Hampel, Judy Piatt, and her two daughters Andrea and Lori. The day following the spraying, dead birds were found inside the arena. Within the next couple of months, 48 horses fell ill, lost their hair, developed open sores, wasted away, and died. In addition, twenty ponies, a number of cats, and the family dog died.

In June 1971, Bliss sprayed the horse arena at Bubbling Springs Ranch in Fenton, Missouri. At the time my son Steven groomed horses stabled there, and he observed the same series of events that occurred at the Shenandoah Stables — signs of illness followed by loss of hair, the development of open running sores, vomiting, wasting away, and then death.

In July of that year, Andrea Piatt was admitted to St. Louis Children's Hospital with severe bleeding and flu-like symptoms. She was diagnosed as suffering from chemical intoxication. This was the first of many trips that she and her sister would make to Children's Hospital where they were treated and tested for several years. The girls were also informed that it was best not to have children because their exposure to dioxin increased the chances of birth defects.

According to a July 21, 1991, article in the St. Louis Post-Dispatch,

Hampel and Piatt claimed to have spent 15 months trailing Bliss' trucks, and in late 1972 they sent a list of sites that he had sprayed to a number of state agencies, including the Missouri Attorney General's office. Among the sites listed was Times Beach.

The governor of the state at that time was Christopher "Kit" Bond, and the state Attorney General was John Danforth. Both later became U. S. Senators. The question is, if what Hampel and Piatt said is true, why did the government wait until 1982, a decade later, before the public was notified and testing begun? According to the Attorney General's office, they have no record of ever being notified.

Judy Piatt eventually filed suit against Bliss and Syntex Agribusiness, the chemical company that owned the plant the dioxin had come from. An out of court settlement was reached for $2.68 million. In November 1992, 381 former residents of Times Beach and other areas also agreed to an out of court settlement with Syntex USA, Syntex Agribusiness, Inc., Northeastern Pharmaceutical & Chemical Company, and Independent Petrochemical Company, for an undisclosed amount. Russell Bliss eventually lost his hauling license and spent eight months in jail and was fined not for spreading the dioxin but for not claiming $27,000 in earnings on his income taxes.

How was it that Russell Bliss, a local waste hauler, came to contaminate so many sites? For that story we have to go back to the late 1960's and Verona, Missouri, which lies about 25 miles southwest of Springfield. The Hoffman-Taff chemical plant, which had manufactured the herbicide Agent Orange there, was acquired by Syntex Agribusiness in November 1969. Earlier that year and on into 1972, Northeastern Pharmaceutical & Chemical Company (NEPACCO) leased a portion of the plant where they manufactured a disinfectant known as hexachlorophene, producing dioxin as a byproduct. Hexachlorophene was eventually banned by the government.

NEPACCO hired Independent Petrochemical Company (IPC) to dispose of its waste. They in turn hired Russell Bliss. Between 1971 and 1972, Bliss transported the waste to St. Louis County where he mixed it with waste oil and disposed of it by spreading it on parking lots, roads, and horse arenas to help reduce dust.

Syntex claims that it first learned about the dioxin waste when they found a tank containing 4,300 gallons of the chemical. They eventually developed a method to decontaminate the waste, and between 1982 and 1984 they and the EPA excavated and contained the dioxin wastes found buried at the James Denney Farm, also near Verona. From 1985 though 1988 Syntex also worked with the EPA to incinerate over 12 million pounds of dioxin-contaminated soil from other southwest Missouri sites.

Because Syntex owned the facilities where the dioxin was created, they were held liable for cleaning up the remaining 27 known dioxin sites in eastern Missouri. The estimated cost to the company is somewhere between $110 to $118 million.

In accordance with the EPA's Record of Decision, published September 29, 1988, and the consent decree signed by Syntex Agribusiness and federal and state officials, Syntex will build a levee around the Times Beach site and operate a temporary incinerator where it will thermally treat dioxin-contaminated soil and other materials. The decontaminated soil will be buried on site. Syntex will also be responsible for razing and disposing of uncontaminated vacant houses and flood debris at Times Beach. These materials will also be buried on site. This agreement clearly states that the incinerator will be a temporary facility and that no hazardous wastes from other states may be incinerated at the site. Upon completion of the project the incinerator will be removed, and after the EPA and the state DNR has certified the area as safe, the 500 acres will be converted to park lands.

All this had been worked out and agreed to by Syntex and federal and state officials, but neither the county citizens nor their County Council were a party to the deal, nor did they approve of the project. On December 31, 1990, U. S. District Judge John Nangle approved the agreement, and cleanup work was scheduled to begin the following March.

As 1991 began to unfold, some progress was being made; relocation had begun and so had the cleanup. Then came news of a series of studies that seemed to suggest that the Times Beach buy-out might not have been necessary. A study reported in the *New England Journal of Medicine* in mid-January was conducted by the National Institute of Occupational Safety and Health in Cincinnati. In twelve U. S. chemical plants, the study showed that production and maintenance workers who worked with dioxin for over a year, and who had blood level averages of 3,600 parts of dioxin per trillion, 20 years later had a 46 percent higher cancer death rate than the general public. However, they found that workers who had blood levels up to 640 parts per trillion, 90 times that of the general public, and had been exposed for less than an year had the same cancer death rate as the general population. This finding, and a similar study of individuals who were exposed to dioxin when a chemical plant in Seveso, Italy, exploded in 1976, seemed to suggest that exposure to low levels of dioxin might not be harmful. Many scientists and environmentalists, however, were quick to point out that it can sometimes take 20 years or more for individuals exposed to carcinogens to develop cancers. It was back in 1985, after testing rats with high levels of dioxin, that the EPA reported that dioxin was among the most toxic chemicals known, and might be linked to a number of cancers.

On May 21, 1991, Dr. Vernon N. Houk, an official with the Centers For Disease Control (CDC) made a shocking announcement at the 25th annual International Conference on Trace Substances in Environmental

Health held in Columbia, Missouri. He stated in a "Dioxin Update" that if he had known back in 1982 what he knew now, he would not have recommended the evacuation of Times Beach. He believed that based on the recent findings, the government's safety standard of one part of dioxin per billion parts of soil was too high.

Of course, Times Beach had readings much higher than one part per billion — in a few cases they were as high as 1,100 parts per billion. But that didn't seem to matter. What followed was the "see, I told you so" chorus, sung by those Times Beach residents who fought relocation, and, of course, the chemical industry who had downplayed the health risk from the beginning. However, others at the conference such as Donald G. Barnes, director of the EPA's science advisory board, felt that while the CDC might have overestimated the danger, it was better to be safe than sorry. He believed that more in-depth studies needed to be made. It was the chemical industry, however, who pushed the government the hardest to conduct more studies on the effects of exposure to low levels of dioxin. On April 10, 1991, the EPA agreed to do just that.

In September 1994, the long-awaited 2,000-page report was published. Instead of downplaying the effects of dioxin, it reinforced the original 1985 report, going so far as to say that dioxin in any amount may lead to such health problems as developmental and reproductive disorders, disruption of hormones, and suppression of the immune system. It now looks as if the chemical industry had shot itself in the foot.

While this report seemed to vindicate the Times Beach evacuation, it only added fuel to the incineration question. Back in 1990, there were two non-binding referendums on the St. Louis City and St. Louis County ballots. Both City and County residents voted on the federal government's plan to store low-level radioactive waste at the Lambert Airport site. That question received an resounding 85 percent "no" vote. In the county they voted on whether to incinerate dioxin at Times Beach. That vote was much closer: about 55 percent no, to 45 percent yes, although in those areas closest to the incineration site, the vote was overwhelmingly no!

While the federal government has backed off on the radiation issue, the state and federal governments had every intention of completing the dioxin cleanup and incineration. In November 1994, the findings of a federal study stated the proposal to burn dioxin-contaminated soils at Times Beach carried minimal health risks. The EPA said that a farm family living within three miles of the incineration who eat food they grow, at the very worst, would have a one-in-a-million chance of getting cancer from the emissions.

It was this report that the state DNR had been waiting for. Thus on December 16, 1994, David Shorr, Director of the DNR, with the blessing of the federal EPA, signed a draft permit allowing the Times Beach incinerator to be built. It was estimated that construction would begin by the end of January and the project would be completed by 1996.

Under the provisions of the consent decree, once the incinerator is built, a test burn using materials similar to dioxin will be made. If it passes, another permit will be issued to test-burn the contaminated materials. If that goes well, the incinerator will begin full-scale operations. It should be noted that this is the only time the incinerator will be tested directly. In the past, both Syntex and the EPA claimed that both burns would meet the "six nines test," which means that 99.9999 percent of the dioxin will be destroyed. Throughout the incineration, the Missouri Department of Health and St. Louis University will be taking and testing blood samples from 75 volunteers near the burn site.

Congressman Jim Talent of the second district didn't approve of the Times Beach incinerator and tried unsuccessfully to get the Congress to halt the project. He and several local environmental action groups, such as the Times Beach Action Group (T-BAG), felt that a newer method that has been used at several other sites would be much safer. The system is called Base-Catalyzed Decomposition (BCD). Like incineration, it uses heat to destroy the dioxin, but because it is a closed system, there are few emissions. Talent has stated that he couldn't understand why the EPA has allowed two similar projects to be postponed while more studies are done, but not Times Beach.

When efforts failed to have Congress put the incineration on hold, attention next centered around Missouri Governor Mel Carnahan, who has the power to reopen the consent decree. The Governor, however, has sided with the EPA and refused to reconsider.

Action then shifted to the St. Louis County Council. From the beginning, the council has opposed the incinerator and has even threatened to close access to the site. At this juncture it looked as if they were totally out of the picture, but then they were reminded that under the consent decree it is up to them to issue an air pollution control permit for the incinerator.

On December 29, 1994, the council, in a 6-0 vote, set an emission level at 0.15 nanograms of dioxin per each cubic meter of air. A nanogram is one-billionth of a gram, slightly below the 99.9999 level the EPA said the incinerator could operate at. Following that vote, Gary Pendergrass, the Syntex Agribusiness project coordinator, warned that the emissions limit could delay the project. In the past, Syntex has stated that any additional cost due to delays might be passed on to taxpayers. The above statement is interesting considering that Syntex said from the start that it would have no problem meeting the six nines standard. At present, this is where the issue stands.

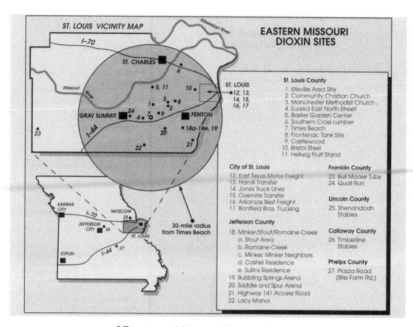

27 eastern Missouri dioxin sites —
Missouri Department of Natural Resources

CEMENT KILNS

As I reflect upon the issue of burning of hazardous waste, I find it interesting that Countians are more upset about an incinerator yet to be built, one that will be operated under strict guidelines and come under great public scrutiny, than they are about the tons of hazardous waste presently being pumped into the air under less stringent regulations. But then few folks, locally and nationally, are informed about the cement kilns that have recently been converted to burn hazardous waste as fuel.

Because of loopholes in federal and state hazardous waste laws, the same permits aren't required nor are kilns monitored to the same degree as regular commercial hazardous waste incinerators. Today about two-thirds of all hazardous waste incinerated is being burned in cement kilns. Missouri has four, the largest number in any state, located in Hannibal, Clarksville, Festus, and Cape Girardeau. Together they burn well over 250,000 tons of waste a year, the highest amount of any state. Missouri cement kilns are also the #1 and #3 emitters of dioxin. River Cement Company of Festus ranks first in the country, and Continental Cement in

Hannibal is third. The Festus plant at present receives and burns waste from 26 states and two foreign countries.

In 1993 the EPA sought a $3.36 million penalty against River Cement for storing and burning violations at its Festus plant. The city of Festus is in Jefferson County, less than 30 miles south of the St. Louis County border. Among the 20 counts charged against River Cement were:

- failure to obtain detailed waste analysis;
- failure to monitor maximum combustion chamber temperature;
- failure to submit a complete and accurate certification of compliance;
- an inadequate closure plan and closure cost estimates;
- illegal storage of hazardous wastes;
- failure to minimize possibility of release of hazardous waste.

There are a number of problems associated with cement kilns used to burn hazardous waste. Because of the intense levels of heat required (2,500 - 3,000 degrees Fahrenheit), virtually all of the mercury found in the waste is vaporized and discharged into the atmosphere uncontrolled. Other toxicants such as lead, cadmium, arsenic, and dioxin are either emitted from the stack, absorbed by dust particles, or actually become part of the cement product.

Because of the relaxed environmental rules, kiln operators are able to offer companies that produce hazardous waste more favorable terms than licensed commercial incinerators. This sideline has become a very profitable by-product of the cement industry. Since the 1980's, their share of the liquid hazardous waste market has also increased from 40 to 60 percent, which annually amounts to 2.5 million tons.

There are also disposal problems related to kiln refuse as well as the increased contamination that can occur when kilns malfunction. So while the Times Beach dioxin incineration has drawn most of the public's attention, chemical waste incineration at nearby cement kilns and the proposed construction of new medical waste incinerators in the metropolitan area will raise health risk questions long after the Times Beach issue has been resolved.

11 - Bridge Over Troubled Waters

The Castlewood cleanup was completed by 1987 at a cost ranging in the millions. And I must say the EPA did an excellent job, leaving the town in a little better shape than when they found it. The contaminated soil is presently being stored in bunkers off Sontag Road, where it will remain until disposed of at Times Beach.

By the mid-1980's, not only was development heading towards Castlewood with "the sound of diesels and a cloud of dust"; it came in a flood. As previously mentioned, the rocky and hilly terrain in large portions of West County had been previously passed over by developers. When I first moved here in 1978, there were few developments west of Highway 141 and Big Bend Road, but by 1990 the area from that point to New Ballwin Road had been largely filled in. With most of the prime land gone, builders began taking to the rugged hillsides in the Kiefer Creek valley.

As early as February 1964, the St. Louis County Planning Commission published a report entitled "Computing Flood Elevations For Small Watersheds In St. Louis County." The report was the outcome of the Planning Commission's master Land Use Plan adopted in 1962. The purpose of the report was to explain the methodology developed by the Planning Commission to determine flood elevations which could be reasonably expected in creeks and streams of St. Louis County. At considerable cost, studies were conducted on all of the watersheds in the County's 500 square miles.

However, what is most interesting about this report is that the Planning Commission used the Kiefer Creek watershed study as their report model. Also, throughout, the report kept coming back to the importance of protecting the floodplains and the areas immediately surrounding them. The report clearly states on page 2 that "One of the basic steps taken in developing the Land Use Plan was to designate and safeguard the floodplains from urban encroachment." Thus, in their original Land Use Plan, the Planning Commission designated the floodplains of area creeks and streams along with their surrounding environs as part of the "Open Space Component."

Also, on the same page, the Commission defined the Open Space Component as land which should be retained in an undeveloped or relatively undeveloped condition. In addition to preserving natural features significant to recreation and aesthetic values, open space areas would include land "too steep for residential or other urban uses,...and those areas containing natural characteristics which will help define and outline communities by breaking up the otherwise undesirable endless sprawl of suburban growth."

Furthermore, the report states on page 3 that "After computing and designating the overflow areas of the creeks and streams it is anticipated that in implementing this phase of the Open Space Component, floodplain zoning will be used as a method of protecting these areas from unwise developments, as well as eliminating the necessity for future expensive flood control projects. This land control will be far more economical for St. Louis County by preserving the drainage areas for the natural function and also by holding public and private expenditures for property protection and personal safety to a minimum."

The report also clearly pointed out the important role that vegetation plays in helping to reduce run-off and erosion. Page 27 states: . . . "It was noted during the field reconnaissance that if urban development in St. Louis County continues to expand in the manner of recent years, much of the natural vegetation coverage will be removed and the overall biological balance will be disrupted. Observations of stream beds by the instrument survey group revealed that below the areas where new subdivisions or other developments were in progress, large deposits of soil matter were transported during heavy rainfalls due to the complete removal of protective vegetation in the subdivision area. This man-made conversion of streams to sediment traps will only aggravate the existing flood problems by producing higher flood elevations." And on page 36: "This . . . study is extremely important because run-off must be anticipated for the future when the proposed development in any one of the watersheds in St. Louis County is completed and all major improvements made."

Finally, on page 61 of that report one can find a diagram for the proposed land use for the Kiefer Creek Watershed through 1980. Under that plan, a neighborhood commercial district would be located north of Manchester Road, with medium residential development north and south of that road but only in the extreme upper reaches of the watershed. As for as the rest of the Kiefer Creek watershed, as stated on page 62, "Due to the scenic quality and the fundamental resources existing, as supplied by nature in plant, animal life, and geological formations, the remaining area in the watershed is designated as Open Space. The value of this woodland drainage area as a medium to conserve water, soil, and wildlife, and as a major educational resource of St. Louis County is unprecedented. Some of this area could serve as future park facilities. The Open Space in this watershed is also a part of a proposed green belt system extending along the complete length of the scenic Meramec River in St. Louis County."

The report also proved to be prophetic when it stated that "These drainage ways were intensively examined because for many years it has been recognized that unless adequate measures are taken to develop an overall plan for control of increased stormwater run-off in St. Louis County, our flood problems will increase and become critical."

The St. Louis County charter requires that the County's General Plan, which included the above study, must be updated every five years, which was done in 1980, 1985, 1990. The 1985 General Plan called for the "systematic preparation of detailed area studies for unincorporated County." As of January 1995, six community area studies have been completed. Each of these area studies took months and even years to complete and involved lots of public input. As in the past, they also recommended strict guidelines to protect the environment and regulate development. However, it should be made clear that they are just that — guidelines. Both the Planning and Zoning Commissions may disregard them, and, of course, the County Council always has the final say.

Well, so much for long-term planning. In spite of all the studies to the contrary, the County Council has approved request after request to rezone three-acre sites downward to as small as quarter-acre lots in the Kiefer Creek watershed. This was done in spite of numerous protests of local residents and their County Councilman Greg Quinn.

Except for where the Spring Branch enters Kiefer Creek in Castlewood, Kiefer Creek is a dry creek bed most of the year. After joining the Spring Branch, the creek flows through the northern half of Castlewood State Park to the Meramec River. During periods of heavy run-off, it now serves as an uncontrolled storm sewer, similar to the River Des Peres.

As the bulldozers tore the great oaks down and scraped the land clean, concrete soon replaced sod. As predicted, with little vegetation left to impede run-off down the steep gradients, erosion and flash flooding increased. New tributaries were formed as the waters rushed down hillsides, along the roadways, and into the creek. It no longer required major storms to flood the creek bottoms. Even when the creek didn't overflow its banks, residents' yards and homes were often flooded by the run-off coming directly from neighboring subdivisions.

Floodwaters also created problems within Castlewood State Park. Twice, between 1992 and 1993, the new bridge being constructed over Kiefer Creek in the park was ripped out and had to be repaired. On September 22, 1993, a major storm hit the area. As the waters ripped through the town, it tore out the New Ballwin bridge and moved several homes off their foundations. As the floodwater ran through the park, it eroded the banks, uprooted trees, and left a trail of human debris in its path.

The loss of the New Ballwin bridge left Kiefer Creek Road as the only access to and from the town for residents' and Metro West's Fire Station # 2. Kiefer Creek Road as it enters Castlewood is very narrow and dangerous. In many places, the shoulder drops off several feet. In fact, there are spots where it's impossible for two school buses to pass each other and impossible for a fire truck to safely pass even an automobile.

You can imagine the reaction of Castlewood residents and the rest of the 12,500 Countians served by Fire Station #2 when they were told that the County had no intention of replacing or even repairing the New Ballwin bridge. Citizens were informed that there just weren't enough funds available. This was particularly upsetting when the citizens learned that the County Council had recently voted to bail out a number of developers who hadn't placed enough money in escrow accounts required to cover the cost of finishing the construction of roads and stormwater systems. In short, the County could find money enough to cover the developers, but not enough to maintain their own roads and bridges. It took months of petition gathering, community meetings, and numerous appearances before the County Council before they finally agreed to repair a little two-lane bridge that crossed a small intermittent creek. Something was seriously wrong.

In February 1994, the County accepted a bid of $62,964 to repair the Kiefer Creek Bridge. The project had been approved by FEMA, which agreed to pay up to 90 percent of the project construction cost. In short, the repair of Kiefer Creek bridge cost the County government a little less than $7,000 — a fraction of what it cost to bail out the developers.

The above experience was just the tip of the iceberg. The Castlewood Improvement Association soon learned that it wasn't only West Countians who were having stormwater and other problems related to re-zoning and development, so were folks who lived in other parts of the unincorporated county.

It was maddening to realize that even when it was obvious that the existing infrastructures of roads and stormwater and sewer systems were already inadequate and over-stressed, rarely was new development denied or postponed until the necessary facilities were upgraded. Again and again the issue came down to the old "you can't stop progress" and "jobs" doctrines. Homeowners and community associations made it clear to the Planning and Zoning Commission and then the Council that it wasn't development they were against but irresponsible development. In addition to speaking out against high-density housing in areas where such re-zoning might increase flooding, we were united against issuing new building permits in areas where the existing infrastructure was already over-stressed.

A growing number of people also favored a tree ordinance which would not only help to control run-off but would also preserve some of the aesthetic qualities of the community. In short, they were echoing the views stated in the Planning Commission's own 1964 report.

Citizens pleaded their case, as the County Executive George Westfall sat mute with arms crossed, head cocked downward as he stared at the table as if he was really bored and had more important things to think about. The really important things — like building a new football stadium.

The one response that Mr. Westfall did direct towards me was that "zoning ordinances were never meant to be permanent." Does that mean that there comes a time when even the County's own long-term planning to protect the health and well-being of the community must be set aside for more important concerns such as economic growth and development? Apparently!

Following the public presentations, someone on the council would politely thank us for expressing our views and inform us that they would take our concerns under advisement. Later, when the issue was voted on, there were usually one or two favorable votes, but the outcome was highly predictable. It seemed obvious to all that our communities were being viewed as commodities. "Greed, greed, greed, the American creed," is alive and well. "Consume, consume, consume, develop, invest — these are the things we love the best."

A sad footnote relating to Kiefer Creek: around noon on April 28, 1994, during a major rainstorm, 36-year-old Molden Pickett, Jr., of Fenton skidded off Kiefer Creek Road south of St. Paul Road into Kiefer Creek. During the storm, the rising waters, at several points, had reached the edge of the road. According to the St. Louis County Police, at about 2:30 p.m. Pickett's body was discovered in 15 feet of water. At the very time the accident is believed to have occurred, I was but a short distant downstream taking pictures of the raging waters, unaware of the tragedy. It's hard to believe that just the previous day the creek's flow at that point was but a trickle. On second thought . . . it's not really so hard to understand.

A NEW WATERSHED

Beginning in 1993, the year of the Great Flood, the Missouri courts began taking a closer look at the rights of the government and developers to inflict pain and suffering on citizens, particularly in the area of altering the natural flow of water. In that year the Missouri Supreme Court handed down a landmark decision in Heins Implement Company vs. Missouri Highway and Transportation Commission. That decision overturned more than one hundred years of legal precedent dealing with the ways in which landowners may divert surface water from their property.

To make a long story short, the court found the Missouri Highway Commission liable for damages to property owned by the Heins Implement Company located near the intersection of U. S. 65 and State Route 10 in Carroll County, Missouri. According to the court, when the Highway Commission constructed a bypass over Route 10, it had not installed a large enough drainage culvert under the bypass to handle floodwaters from Wakenda Creek. As a consequence, water not only backed up onto the Heins property as it had in the past, it now often flooded Heins's buildings with up to 30 inches of water.

Based on past decisions, many observers felt that the Highway Commission would prevail, but this time the court ruled that "the common enemy doctrine no longer reflects the appropriate rule in situations involving surface water run-off." In its place the court adopted a "doctrine of reasonable use."

In the past the "common enemy doctrine" only required upstream landowners to act with some degree of care when discharging surface water onto lower-lying property. The downstream owners also had considerable freedom to divert water off of their property. The court came to the conclusion that the doctrine was no longer practical and had outlived its usefulness.

The court also said that landowners who needlessly or negligently injure a neighbor's property must pay for the resulting damages. On May 10, 1994, a year following the Heins case, a Circuit Court jury in Hillsboro awarded Gene and Wanda Lambrich a $3 million judgment against Fred Weber, Inc. The Lambrichs owned and operated Shady Valley Park and Pool, Inc., which had two commercial fishing lakes that they claimed were ruined due to Weber's negligence. Their business is located between the old and new Missouri Highway 21 bridges just north of the Meramec River. The lawyer for the plaintiff stated that when Weber received the contract to build the new highway in 1987, he was instructed to take proper measures to ensure that mud from the project didn't end up in the lakes. The attorney informed the jury that the only action Weber had taken was to spend less than $300 on straw and fencing, both of which were quickly washed away. The jury agreed that Weber was indeed responsible for the siltation and fish kills.

In reviewing the above court decisions, it seems obvious that the rulings would apply to a number of other types of cases. A few examples would be levees that cause flooding on neighboring properties both across the water course and downstream, man-made or altered drainage areas, and improperly designed, maintained, or failed retention ponds and other stormwater systems.

In October 1994, encouraged by the Heins decision, the trustees of the Indian Tree subdivision in West County, along with residents Roger and Phyllis Shaw and David and Darlene Roby, filed a lawsuit in St. Louis County Circuit Court against Raleigh, Givens, Maynes Development Company and Schroeder Homes, Inc., the developers of the Highland Summit subdivision which lies above the Indian Tree development. The suit claims that when the developers cleared and graded the Highland Summit property, they altered the natural drainage of the area. The plaintiffs claim that since June 30, 1994, run-off has flowed down from the

Highland Summit development onto the Shaws' and Robys' property. In so doing, it cut a gully across the Shaw property and deposited silt in both yards, killing lawns and flowers. At times portions of their yards were covered with 10 inches of water, which damaged the foundation of the Shaw house. The suit asks for a court injunction to stop the stormwater damage as well as compensatory and punitive damages. That case is still pending.

* * *

SAVE THE TREES

Save the trees, save the trees,
Save the trees in the county,
St. Louis, Missouri.

Save the trees, save the trees,
One for you and one for me,
Then all we can for our posterity.

* * *

A year prior to the above lawsuit, when the plan for the Highland Summit development was being passed through the County Council, several West Countians requested the Council to conduct a tree inventory and preserve vegetation to help prevent the runoff and erosion problems forecasted by the professional forester hired to review this site plan. The developer himself came up with the figure of 51 percent, and the Council passed a resolution that 51 percent of the existing vegetation be preserved. Actually, what the individuals wanted was for the County Council to establish a county-wide tree ordinance.

In January 1993, County Councilman John Shear of the First District and Greg Quinn of the Seventh set up an ad hoc Tree Ordinance Committee. Ten representatives served on the committee, two each from North, South, and West County, and four at-large members representing the business community. Stephanie Lickerman, who along with Maryanne Simmons had pushed for the committee, was one of the West County representatives.

The committee spent nine months reviewing existing tree ordinances, held public meetings, and met with representatives from MSD, cable companies, utilities, and the Home Builder's Association. The latter group suggested that while certain new regulations dealing with sidewalks and

107

streets were needed to preserve trees, they wanted no replanting nor preservation ordinance. What they asked for was trust; they wanted to be trusted to do the right thing.

On September 7, 1993, the committee submitted a draft outline to the county's legal department for review. As far as any of the members know, the proposal was never reviewed; no report was ever made. There were several requests to revive it, but without results.

The following year the County Council also set up a series of three stormwater hearings. There were representatives from the MSD, highway department, homeowner associations, etc. Everyone was given a chance to express their views. After the final meeting was held, there was no analysis, no summary, and no recommendations were published. Like the Tree Ordinance Committee, it seemed a terrible waste of time.

* * *

WILD ABOUT WILDWOOD

We're just wild about Wildwood
And the wild things are wild about us.
We're all wild about Wildwood
because we're gonna protect our own stuff!

* * *

Long before the tree ordinance and stormwater hearings, a number of West Countians had already decided that they had had enough. On December 18, 1992, after a year of work, they sent 2,500 signatures and a 112-page plan of intent to the St. Louis County Boundary Commission. The petition asked the commission to place the question of the incorporation of Wildwood on the ballot.

The proposal said that the petitioners wanted to "form a local government, to be known as Wildwood, to control their own destiny with a minimum of government and yet protect the quality of life which they have chosen." If approved, the new town would elect a mayor and two aldermen from each of eight wards. The petition implied that it would limit high-density commercial development and adopt zoning ordinances and tree-preservation regulations more stringent than the county's ordinances. The proposal also said that to limit the size of government, it planned to contract out most of its public services.

If approved by the Boundary Commission and the voters, the 67-square mile area would become the largest municipality in St. Louis

County — even larger than the City of St. Louis. The proposed area also includes prime parcels of state and county greenways, including Babler State Park, Rockwoods Reservation, and Greensfelder County Park. Roughly, the community's boundaries would be set at the Franklin County line on the west, Interstate 44 and Eureka to the south, Ellisville and Clarkson Valley to the east, Chesterfield and the Missouri River to the north.

Under state law, passed in 1989, the St. Louis Boundary Commission reviews all proposals for incorporation. The commission is empowered to decide if proposed new communities are capable of being self-sustaining and whether their incorporation would be injurious to neighboring communities.

After reviewing the petitions and proposal for incorporation, the Boundary Commission denied the request to place the issue on the ballot, stating that an area of such size (with fewer that 17,000 residents) would lack the financial base necessary to provide community services. This was particularly true, the commission said, if, as their proposal stated, the community planned to limit high-density housing and commercial development. Following the commission's finding, the petitioners appealed their case to the Missouri Supreme Court. In May 1994, the court ruled that the state law establishing the St. Louis Boundary Commission was unconstitutional.

The court ruled that the state law that set up the Boundary Commission was in violation of Article VI Section 8 of the state constitution. Section 8 requires the state to pass uniform laws for each of the state's four classes of counties. In short, the court found that St. Louis County was the only first-class county in the state, where state law requires a Boundary Commission to approve a proposal for incorporation before it can be placed on the ballot. Thus, the law creating the Boundary Commission was declared unconstitutional.

On July 14, 1994, councilman Greg Quinn, who represented the Seventh District, introduced a bill before the County Council calling for a vote on the incorporation of Wildwood on November 8. John A. Ross, the County Counselor, urged the Council not to act until the Circuit Court passed judgment on several legal questions pertaining to the proposed incorporation. For one, following the Boundary Commission refusal to place the Wildwood issue on the ballot, both the cities of Ellisville and Chesterfield moved to annex portions of the area. Also, both the County Executive and Counselor, like the now defunct commission, held that Wildwood would not have an adequate tax base needed to prove minimum services. Thus, at the next Council meeting, July 28, a majority of the Council voted not to place the issue on the November ballot.

On November 5, Circuit Court Judge Kenneth M. Romines ruled that the Wildwood issue should be placed on the February 7 Ballot. In his ruling, he stated that "Nothing in the statute authorizes the county to substitute its judgment for the voter's as to whether the proposed incorporation is feasible and beneficial." The county government as well as the cities of Chesterfield and Ellisville appealed the judge's ruling.

Within a week of Judge Romines's decision, the Citizens Opposed to Wildwood organization began a major fund-raising campaign. They were successful in receiving large pledges from the Home Builders Association of Greater St. Louis. As for the County Executive's feelings about the drive to incorporate Wildwood, his response quoted by the Post-Dispatch back in October was "Nothing's happening out there that hasn't happened in other suburban locales here." Precisely, was the response of Wildwood proponents.

The main battle lines pertaining to the Wildwood incorporation would be drawn around the question of whether Wildwood would be financially solvent. The opposition claimed that by the end of their first year, Wildwood could be in debt by as much as $1.5 million. The opposition had hired Donald Phares, a professor of economics and public policy at the University of Missouri at St. Louis, to make a cost analysis of the proposed community. Phares estimated that the above shortfall would cost each household $262. Phares said that the Wildwood group hadn't taken into account 39 miles of roads the county was now planning to add to the new city if approved by voters.

However, Ron Marcantano, a budget expert and Wildwood supporter, retorted that sales, utilities, and other taxes would bring in more money than originally projected. Thus, when the Wildwood group released their proposed budget, they projected a balance of $165,815 at the end of 1995 and a $1.17 million balance by the end of 1996. These figures were produced by French, McGowan, an accounting firm employed by several local municipalities to review their budgets. The "figures don't lie, but liars figure" debate would continue up until the day of the election.

February 7 finally arrived, and when the votes were counted, there were 4,746 yes votes to 3,059 no votes. Though the opponents had spent over $40,000, nearly two times as much as the proponents, the measure still passed by 61 percent. Wildwood supporters were jubilant. On election night, 200 people crammed into the home of Charles and Myrna Parsley to celebrate their victory. Sue Cullinane, one of the driving forces in the Wildwood campaign, reminded everyone that no matter how much money the opposition spent, it couldn't obliterate "all this devastation from irresponsible development."

But while they celebrated, a little black cloud hovered above. The Missouri Supreme Court had yet to rule on the appeals, and might not until the year's end. In the meantime, the Planning and Zoning Commission continued to receive and review re-zoning requests for the Wildwood area.

After the celebration, the Wildwood group again urged the County Executive and the County Council to drop the county's appeal and allow the city to begin functioning as soon as possible. Under state law, after incorporation has been approved by the voters, the Council is required to appoint a temporary mayor and city council until the new city can elect its own officials.

On February 9, 1995, County Executive Westfall said that while he would not drop the suit, he would ask the Missouri Supreme Court to speed up its consideration of the county's legal challenge to the City of Wildwood. The County's position was that a Circuit Court judge could not usurp the council's authority to decide if a proposed city has a large enough tax base to provide necessary public services. At that same council meeting, Westfall asked the County Planning Commission and County Council to hold up approval of any new subdivisions proposed for the Wildwood area that were submitted after the February 7 vote.

Councilman Greg Quinn criticized Westfall's position, pointing out that his proposed moratorium on new development did not apply to the more than 1,400 homes, condominiums, and apartments that were pending prior to the election.

On March 8, Circuit Court Judge Robert Lee Campbell heard a plea from the Wildwood attorneys asking him to have the county declare Wildwood a city and appoint its interim officials. After meeting with attorneys from both sides, the judge placed a freeze on future rezoning in the Wildwood area until a decision was reached. However, the judge did say that the county may approve site plans and issue building permits to developers who had filed before November 5, 1994, the date Romines placed Wildwood on the ballot.

At the following day's County Council meeting, the Council, as predicted, added an additional 39 miles of roads that Wildwood would have to maintain if their incorporation was approved. Quinn was the only councilman to vote against the measure, saying it was a move on the part of the County Council to discourage future incorporations and annexations.

At this time relations between the County and Wildwood proponents remain strained. The County Council continues their appeal and processing of building permits in the Wildwood area. The state Supreme Court had set May 9 as the day arguments on the Wildwood appeal will be heard. But then on May 4th, the Missouri Supreme Court sent the Wildwood case back to the local appellate courts on the grounds that the County's case was null and void due to the passage of proposition A, in April. By approving proposition A the state constitution was amended so that the state legislature could pass laws that pertain only to St. Louis, Jefferson, and St. Charles counties, thus voiding that section of the Missouri constitution that had previously caused the demise of the Boundary Commission.

In another important matter, the Missouri Court of Appeals on March 29 dealt the St. Louis Metropolitan Sewer District a major blow, in a 2-1 decision ordering the sewer district to refund $40 million to 420,000 of its customers in St. Louis City and County. In 1993, the Missouri Supreme Court ruled that the Sewer District's 1992 fee increase without voter approval violated the Hancock amendments. The MSD had based its 1992 fee increase on the state Supreme Court's 1991 decision in Keller vs. Marion County Ambulance District. In that decision, the court implied that the Hancock amendment applied to taxes, not user fees. But in 1993, the Supreme Court ruled that the MSD rate hike should have been voted on. A St. Louis Circuit Court ordered a refund, MSD appealed, and the appellate court upheld the lower court's ruling. After taking some time to think the matter over, MSD has decided to appeal the Circuit Court's ruling to the Missouri Supreme Court.

To make matters worse, the 1993 $73 million rate increase is also being challenged in St. Louis Circuit Court, and based on the current rulings, it too might be declared unconstitutional and a refund ordered. In short, without a voter-approved fee increase, the MSD will be bankrupt. Then the question will once again be, "St. Louie, Louie, Louie, Louie, what you gonna do about your stink, a'dink, a'dink, a'dinky-doo?"

This is the present state of affairs in St. Louis County regarding Wildwood incorporation, MSD, and other important issues. As I write this, it is mid-April 1995, and this weekend St. Louisans along with the rest of the country will be celebrating the 25th anniversary of our country's first Earth Day. And, while we have made some real progress, Mother Nature is still being taxed to the breaking point. It seems as if the United States Congress, state government, big business, and property rights advocates are about to issue the coup de grace that will undo the gains made over the last quarter century.

Once again — "these are the times that try men's souls." The problem is we still want it all, don't we? Jobs, progress, economic growth, open space, etc., etc., etc.! Homo sapiens — the only species who refuses to live according to Mother Nature's basic tenets.

* * *

MOTHER NATURE'S NOT FEELING WELL

Mother Nature's not feeling well.
Quiet please!
She's got a terrible headache,
She's feeling kind of weak in the knees.

She just needs a little vacation,
A whole lot of rest.
She's been worn to a frazzle
Just trying to do her best.

To keep her family fed and clothed,
That's her number one goal.
But the more of us and the bigger we get
the more and more we grow.

Give me this!
Give me that!
Up the GNP!
She's getting frustrated
I think she's getting peeved.

Maybe she'll stir up a tornado,
Disease or pestilence.
You better get down on your knees, man,
And repent, repent, repent.

Because, Mother Nature's not feeling well.
She's critically ill
And if she don't recover
There won't be a need . . .
No, there won't be a need
For a will.

* * *

Waste Disposal at the Weldon Spring Site

The engineered disposal facility, or cell, to be constructed in the chemical plant area will provide long-term isolation of the site's waste material. The footprint of the facility will cover approximately 72 acres. The average height of the structure will be 40 feet and approximately 1.1 million cubic yards of waste can be placed. These conceptual drawings show how the cell will look during various phases of its construction and completion.

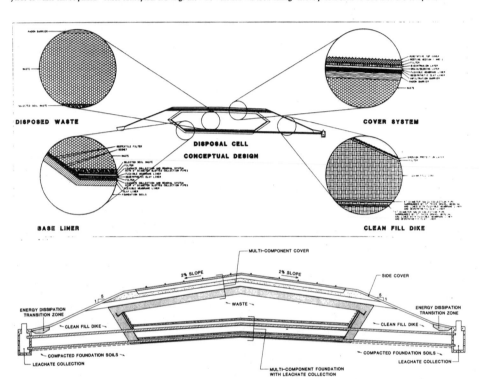

CONCEPTUAL DISPOSAL CELL CROSS SECTION WITH CLEAN FILL DIKE

NOT TO SCALE

Planned waste disposal at the Weldon Spring site.

PART V

THE QUEST

    As I awaited the outcome of the Wildwood Issue, I tried to return to my previous work. But it's hard to switch gears. Up until the time I got involved in *STORIES AND SONGS,* I had been working on a book called *Mike and Mingo.* It centers around the story of a young man named Mike Koler who helps raise and then trains a young red-tailed hawk, Mingo, at the Raptor Rehabilitation and Propagation Project (now the World Bird Sanctuary) to survive in the wild. In part, the story focuses on the history of the evolution of humans as predators and their relationships with other predators. It points out how the wolf, the eagle, and others became our mentors, and how after we moved on to become cultivators and domesticators, we turned on our former kindred spirits. Last, it looks at how we are beginning to come full circle.

12 - The Medicine Wheel

Some years ago, while researching the history of the First Americans, I came across the beautiful story of the Medicine Wheel. The Medicine Wheel was used by the Plains Indians to explain their relationship to one another and the other things that make up their universe.

The wheel is usually laid out as a circle of small stones. Each stone represents a thing or individual. A smaller circle of stones is placed in the center of the wheel. Radiating outward from its center towards north, south, east, and west are other stones representing other entities. According to the Indians, each of these directions is a power point on the wheel and is represented by a certain color as well as a spirit animal with special gifts. To the north is the color white and the buffalo, which represents wisdom. To the south is the color green and the mouse, representing innocence. To the east is yellow and the eagle, representing illumination (vision). To the west is the color black and the bear, representing introspection, the ability to look within oneself.

The Plains Indians believe that each person starts life at one of these points and will grow up with its gift. Thus, a person born under the sign of the buffalo, the North, will have great wisdom, but will start out lacking in the other three great gifts. They believe that one's goal in life should be to know one's beginning place and then to learn the other gifts through the study of nature and from others. The latter is often done through the telling of tribal stories in which plants and animals, who reflect human emotions, are often the main or supporting characters.

When one has come full circle, they believe, one will have become a whole person. Furthermore, when one has achieved that goal, it is believed that he or she will never be surprised or feel threatened by the decisions and actions of others. In short, they will be in complete harmony with the universe.

It's easy to see the important role that animal spirits play in the lives of the Indians. Throughout most of North America, each Indian nation and generally individual tribes within each nation had a spirit animal that guided them. Individual tribes were then broken down into family clans, which might also be represented by a special spirit animal. Within each clan, each individual, after having completed his or her vision quest, had their own individual spirit animal.

It should be made clear here that the tribe, the clan, the individual, do not actually worship these animals as gods but view them as kin ("brother

116

bear") and/or spirit guides. Also the Indian legends and stories that incorporate these animals are metaphorical, not to be taken literally.

Another thing about the Indian culture that I think is quite wonderful is that unlike the white culture, each Indian name has special personal meaning. In most tribes, as the individual grows and develops, his or her name changes. For example, a boy will start out with a baby's name; as he develops his skills he will receive a young warrior's name; after he has successfully completed his first raid, he will receives his full warrior's name.

In addition to the Medicine Wheel the Indians made sacred tribal and individual shields. Animal hides were stretched into the shape of the Medicine Wheel and painted in the appropriate colors and signs that told the story of the tribe as well as each man's past, present, and dreams. The personal shield was seen as mirror image of the individual and a constant reminder of who he was and his place within the tribe, the clan, and the universe. The shields were adorned with eagle feathers, animal fur, and other special items. These personal shields were placed outside their lodges so all could know the individuals. They were also carried with them when they went afield.

I see this sense of awareness as one of the biggest voids in our present American culture. That void I think helps to explain the confusion and lack of direction shared by many of our youth and adults today. In our artificial world, so many souls seem lost in time and place.

During the last couple years that I taught, for me to get to know my students better and for them to know themselves, I had my homeroom students make their own personal shields. I asked them to pick an animal that best represented their own personality, and then, sometimes with the help of the class, they chose their own name. Then they would incorporate it all together on their shields using symbolic images and colors. It was lots of fun, and I hope a meaningful experience for them.

I, of course, had to come up with my own Indian name and shield. The name I chose is "Lone Paddle Rainbow Chaser," and my shield shows a canoeist hooked up with a jumping trout beneath a rainbow.

Of all the animal spirits mentioned in the traditional culture of the Plains Indians, the one that best represents their dreams is the eagle. As hunters they emulated the eagle. One earned the right to wear its feathers not by birth, but through acts of bravery, skill, and good deeds. Since our first beginnings, I suspect human beings have always wanted to fly with the eagles.

THE DREAM

As for myself, I can remember a recurring dream I had since early childhood. In that dream I would leap into the air and vigorously flap my arms, glide a few feet, and than crash to the ground. The dream was always the same, except each time I'd go just a inch or two farther. This dream continued well into adulthood.

One night some years back, I dreamed I leapt into the air, but this time I didn't come crashing to the ground as in the past. Instead, I flew right out an open window and soared high above, free to go wherever I wanted. After a brief sojourn, I returned by way of the same open window and went back to sleep. I awoke refreshed, and that was the last time I ever had that dream.

I was puzzled by that experience and would have passed the whole thing off as just a silly dream if it hadn't been so much a part of my being. Later, when I discovered the story of the Medicine Wheel with its spirit animals and their gifts, I wondered if it is possible that the dream represented a major turn on the wheel towards ILLUMINATION. That would be nice.

Bald Eagle.

* * *

WISH I WAS AN EAGLE

Wish I was an eagle
Wish I could fly
Wish I was an eagle so high in the sky.
If I was an eagle I could look down and see
Truth, and love, and life,
more clearly.

Some say I'm not an eagle
Tell me I can't fly
Then, if I'm not an eagle
Be silly to try and to try.
"There's no magic to keep you off the ground
Better keep your dreams, boy,
Earthy bound!"

Don't they know I'm a fledgling
Still got soft white down
If you help me
I think I'll leave the ground.

But I'm gonna need pure water
Fill up all my thirst-
(For truth and knowledge)
Gonna need
clear blue skies
better see my universe.

Gonna need lots of sunshine
Feel it in my heart
See it in your eyes.

Teach me the things we now know on earth
It will help me to fly.

Wish we all were eagles
I wish we all could fly
Wish we all were eagles
So high in the sky!
If we were all eagles
We could look down and see
Truth, and love, and life, more clearly.

* * *

Third verse not included on recording.

119

Castlewood dioxin cleanup.

PART VI

UPDATE

Loyalty to petrified opinion never broke a
chain or freed the human soul.
— Mark Twain

On July 27, 1995, 14 individuals were arrested when they crossed a police barricade at the Times Beach incinerator site. Over one hundred protesters were present on that day. Many of them carried placards and banners as they marched and chanted in the 92-degree heat while their comrades sat with their hands cuffed behind them. And behind them was a wall of 17 County police officers who stood at attention as they guarded the bridge that leads to the incinerator, still under construction. Completion and test-burn should take place around November 1995.

I was present on that day and what impressed me most about the protesters, and those who were arrested in particular, was that most were local folks who hadn't ever been arrested for anything worst than a traffic ticket. While those arrested remained calm throughout the ordeal, it was obvious that though some were scared, they had resolved to make their stand. They were learning about civil disobedience, hands on, up close, and personal.

To my right, I heard a megaphone directing comments towards the police and EPA officials. It was my son Steve, co-founder of the Times Beach Action Group (T-BAG) and the primary organizer of the protest. He and his group had spent months gathering information on the Internet and were working closely with Pat Costner, a Greenpeace scientist who through the Freedom of Information Act had gained access to the prematurely released EPA study on the dioxin blood levels of residents living near the Vertac dioxin incinerator in Jacksonville, Arkansas.

13 - In the Course of Human Events

TIMES BEACH INCINERATOR

On May 2, 1995, Dr. Morris Cranmer traveled to St. Louis and informed the St. Louis County Dioxin Monitoring Committee that the blood levels of residents living in and around the Vertac site had dropped in the three years it was in operation. However, after Costner had gained access to the raw data, Cranmer quickly reversed himself and said that after reviewing the data he discovered he had used the wrong mathematical analysis and now admits that blood levels of TCDD, the most toxic form of dioxin, along with several other types, had actually increased.

Dr. Cranmer is an interesting case study, for he began his relationship with the Arkansas State Department of Health in 1988 in a most inauspicious way. On February 5 of that year, he was convicted on two counts of fraud for making false statements to two banks from which he borrowed $10 million. The loans were guaranteed by the Farmers Home Administration and were to be used to build a toxicological laboratory in Jefferson County, Arkansas.

In 1983 Cranmer defaulted on the loans leaving the Farmers Home Administration to pay off $9.5 million of the $10 million loan. The court found Cranmer guilty of having diverted the funds intended for the Jefferson County project to a number of properties he owned in the Little Rock area.

On the day Cranmer was convicted Dr. Joycelyn Elders, then the Arkansas State Department of Health Director and later the U. S. Surgeon General, who knew Cranmer, requested that instead of serving time in prison he be allowed to perform community service for the Department of Health. U. S. District Judge Henry Woods consented to Elders' request and ordered Cranmer to perform 9 months of public service for the state of Arkansas while living in a Little Rock halfway house for federal prisoners.

Following Cranmer's community service, Elders appointed him the chief investigator who would monitor and analyze the dioxin exposure study at the Vertac incinerator. The study was to determine whether dioxin levels increased in local residents during the time that the incinerator was in operation. Thus, since 1991 Cranmer has received over $139,400 in federal funds — a great American success story of how when you're down and out in Little Rock you can turn a lemon into lemonade, or as the Arkansas Democrat - Gazette pointed out in a July 8, 1995, article, how you can convert pluses into minuses.

According to the Gazette, "The study came under scrutiny . . . when it was learned that Cranmer changed the numbers on dioxin levels detected in residents' blood samples taken in 1991 and 1994." It was those figures that were sent to the Arkansas Department of Health peer review panel, which is a requirement under federal law. The panel, however, failed to catch the error. Thus, from March through May, Cranmer maintained that dioxin levels had declined in Jacksonville residents — that was before Pat Costner acquired copies of the report, which could have been the reason Cranmer decided to take another look-see. After reviewing what he called bad math, Cranmer changed his position and said that dioxin levels had "increased slightly." What is slightly? Between 1991 and 1994 blood samples drawn from 34 Jacksonville residents who lived within 1,300 yards of the Vertac incinerator showed a 7.9 percent increase in dioxin, and in the control group from Mabelvale the levels actually went up 12 percent! Why would levels increase in the control group? It could be that there are two waste incinerators in that area.

So, what is the implication of these increases? No one can say for sure, but the federal government's 1994 study, if you remember, concluded that any level of exposure to dioxin can be dangerous to the reproductive and immune systems. But what is significant here is that the blood samples show that there is indeed a correlation between incineration and increased blood levels of dioxin.

The above story is but another footnote in the continuing saga. While the protest continued to keep the issue in the public eye, from a legal standpoint, the fight over the County's air quality permit that was issued February 2, 1995, has become the focus of the controversy. In May, Syntex Corporation and the U. S. Environmental Protection Agency filed a suit in Federal Court charging that the County's air permit was invalid because it goes beyond the requirements of the 1988 consent decree that approved the Times Beach incinerator. In July, the County countered by saying that while federal law does not normally require that such a cleanup receive local government approval, Syntex and the EPA agreed in the 1988 consent decree to obtain the appropriate local permits.

Several points should be made here. One is that the County's 0.15 nanogram limit on dioxin emissions is actually lower than the 99.9999 percent level that both Syntex and the EPA have claimed from day one they could achieve. Secondly, as far back as January 24, 1993, in an article titled "State Firm On Rule For Incinerator/ 99.9999 Of Dioxin Must Be Destroyed," the Post-Dispatch quoted Linda James, then the Missouri DNR dioxin coordinator, as saying that International Technology Corporation, which had been awarded the contract to burn the dioxin-contaminated soil, would be "required to demonstrate six-nines destruction" before it would get a permit to burn dioxin.

So, if the County passed an ordinance that requires dioxin at Times Beach to be burned at levels below government standards — below what the EPA, DNR and Syntex said they could — what's the problem, and why the court case? The problem is that no incinerator has ever been able to burn dioxin at the "six nines" level and the EPA knew it as far back as 1985. According to the same Post article, back in the late 1980's the EPA hired Midwest Research Institute located in North Carolina to conduct field studies on dioxin incinerators. They tested eight incinerators and found none were able to destroy dioxin at the 99.9999 percent level. This also proved to be the case at the Jacksonville incinerator when they started burning dioxin back in 1991. At Jacksonville, as was the case with the eight other incinerators tested, only the substitute materials used in the test burns achieved a "six nines" burn. The best any of them could do with the real stuff was 99.96 percent.

In spite of their own data, the EPA has always maintained that the substitute material is more difficult to destroy than dioxin — a position that disputes their own findings. Thus, I would conclude that like Dr. Cranmer, the EPA and Syntex are guilty of fraud on two counts — one by maintaining that they would have no difficulty in achieving a "six nines" dioxin burn and, two, that it is more difficult to achieve a "six nines" burn with the substitute material than with dioxin.

Following the Jacksonville incident, the EPA simply changed the rules. According to William Sanjour, an EPA policy analyst for the Office of Solid Waste, Sylvia Lowrance, the office director, issued a memo that instructed EPA waste managers on how to issue permits to operate hazardous waste incinerators which didn't meet minimum performance standards. According to Sanjour the memo suggested that permits could be issued if the incinerators meet the "six nines" rule when burning the substitute material, even though that might not be the case when burning dioxin.

Thus, it should now be perfectly clear why Syntex and the EPA went to court — the County called their bluff and they couldn't ante-up! On August 15, U. S. District Judge John F. Nangle handed down his decision. He ruled that the county's new air pollution ordinance can regulate "conventional" pollutants emitted from the Times Beach Incinerator but not dioxin. He stated that the ordinance is "inapplicable" because it is inconsistent with the consent decree and federal law. Since the ruling, the County has been reviewing the judge's order and has made no official response. So, to date, that's where things stand.

Of all the issues covered in this work none were more difficult to understand and get a handle on than this one. Honest folks — layman and scientist, local, state, federal governments and agencies — can honestly

124

disagree on what is the best method of dealing with the dioxin problem. In fact, in the past I have viewed the dioxin incineration as one of our lesser environmental evils. But, as I dug deeper and deeper into the issue, my grandfather's words of wisdom keep coming to mind: "The only way to deal with people is to be honest and fair" and "In time all liars and cheats are found out." And there lies the bigger issue.

Throughout it has been the Countians, particularly those who were exposed in the past and those to be exposed in the future, who have been left out of the loop. Those most affected are the ones who had the least say. As I see it, from day one it was a done deal. It was a quick fix deal between the three major parties financially committed, one way or another, to cleaning up the mess: the EPA superfund, the state DNR and Syntex Agribusiness. And, interestingly, somehow Russell Bliss' financial responsibility for the disaster has been all but forgotten.

It seems obvious that even though they know they couldn't do what they said they could, none of the above parties wanted to consider any alternatives. One, to scrap the incinerator and invest in another system would be more costly, and secondly, if the incinerator was scrapped and a different procedure was decided upon, Syntex, who is required to pay for the bulk of the cleanup, might sue for breach of contract. Again, because of the way the whole issue was handled from the start, the real losers are the citizens, honesty, and democratic principles. *Salus populi suprema lex esto* — Let the welfare of the people be the supreme law!

CEMENT KILNS

As mentioned earlier, the number one emitters of dioxin in the country are cement kilns used to burn hazardous waste. Our state ranks first in the numbers of kilns that burn hazardous waste and in the amount of dioxin they burn. Because kiln operators fear that the EPA will soon impose more stringent controls, they have been working through Missouri Senator John Ashcroft to bring an end to the EPA's current system of studying the indirect health risks posed by gases and particles emitted from these kilns. Ashcroft has said that the combustion strategy announced by the EPA in May 1993, which would more closely regulate hospitals, cement kilns and other operations that burn waste, is too burdensome. In May, he and Senator Trent Lott of Mississippi suggested to Senate Majority Leader Bob Dole that the language in the regulatory overhaul bill should prevent the EPA from using risk studies in issuing permits unless the standards are "scientifically vetted through the rule making process." Roger Pryor, Executive Director of the Missouri Coalition of the Environment, responded to that suggestion, as quoted by the Post-Dispatch on July 14, "I gather the definition of sound science is whatever the industry agrees with."

125

Kiln operators are also seeking help from Missouri Senator Christopher Bond who heads the Senate subcommittee that oversees EPA appropriations. One subcommittee proposal would bar the EPA from spending money for studies, again under its combustion strategy, without first developing formal rules, which could mean a delay of six months to several years. Thus, there are assaults on a number of fronts to thwart efforts to bring cement kilns that burn hazardous wastes up to par with commercial waste incinerators, and Missouri's Senators Bond and Ashcroft could be instrumental in pulling it off. More about Congress and the State Legislature later.

MSD

Of all the topics discussed in this work, the most financially tenuous issue involves the Metropolitan Sewer District. Back in April, the Missouri Court of Appeals ordered MSD to refund $40 million collected in 1992-3 as an new rate increase. MSD based that increase on a Missouri Supreme Court decision (Keller vs. Marion County Ambulance District) which indicated that the Hancock amendment, which requires local tax increases to be approved by voters, did not apply to rate increases. MSD was sued and the Missouri Court of Appeals sided with the plaintiff and thus ordered the refund. MSD has since appealed the ruling to the State Supreme Court, which to date hasn't ruled on the matter.

Also being challenged was the sewer district's 1993 $73 million rate increase. However, on July 21, 1995, MSD finally won one —at least for the time being. On that day St. Louis Circuit Court Judge Thomas F. McGuire ruled in favor of the sewer district. However, the plaintiff appealed its decision to the Missouri Court of Appeals. Presently both of these cases remain unresolved, so the possibility of MSD going bankrupt is still very real.

MSD's financial problems are just the tip of the iceberg. At the heart of the problem is an archaic system which is in desperate need of repair and retooling. When established by the voters in 1954, the sewer district inherited the city's crude system that dated all the way back to the days of Samuel Curtis. Some of the old trunk sewers are now nearing the 150-year mark. In recent years there has been an increasing incidence of St. Louis streets collapsing as the sewers give way. Just recently the Forest Park restoration project was made public. The projected cost for restoration is $70 million of which $20 million will be needed for sewers. In addition to the above, MSD has estimated the cost of needed stormwater projects throughout the district at $600 million.

On August 2, 1995, approximately 100 basements in St. Louis near South Grand Boulevard and Bates Streets were flooded when 1.5 inches of rain fell within 15 minutes. During the storm, the waters reached such heights that several individuals had to be rescued by boat. At a local meeting residents complained to MSD about the failure of the $1.2 million pump system that MSD installed three years ago. John Koeper, Executive Director of the sewer district, said that the pumping system wasn't equipped to handle such heavy stormwaters. According to Koeper, without the pumps, flooding would have been much worst.

The problem is that in most of St. Louis City, unlike most of the County, storm waters are diverted into the sewer system. Koeper said that the only solution to the above problem is to construct a stormwater system that flows directly into the Mississippi River. To take care of just the above area would cost an estimated $27 million.

Meanwhile, in West County it was more of the same. Not only were area homes and roads flooded on August 2, but again on the 6th and the 15th. Though Kiefer Creek overflowed its banks, the new bridge held. The area of greatest property damage was within the Fish Pot Creek watershed. The creek begins near the intersection of Clayton and Clarkson Roads in Ellisville and flows southeast through the heart of Ballwin and Manchester before entering the Meramec River east of Castlewood State Park. Residents living near the intersection of Ries Road and Oak just North of Castlewood State Park were among the hardest hit. As in South St. Louis, yards and basements were flooded with several feet of water. The flooding also caused traffic problems as automobiles were stalled at a number of points along the creek's course. Residents protested at the Ballwin City Hall on August 14. Mayor Ed Montgomery informed residents that the creek wasn't the City's responsibility and even if it was they didn't have the money to fix it.

Back in 1986, MSD took over control of the creek from the St. Louis County Sewer Company but is responsible only for the sanitary sewers in the area. As is the case throughout most of the less developed areas of the County, there is no stormwater sub-district serving the area. While new developments in the County are now required to build retention ponds, like pumping stations they are limited in their ability to hold back run-off, and as was pointed out earlier, they to can add to the problems. Also, MSD has no jurisdiction over the widening of existing roads or new road construction, which as pointed out in the Heins case, can also create stormwater problems. Many residents believe that the recent widening of Clarkson Road is at least partially responsible for the current problem along Fish Pot Creek.

At present MSD services 400,000 City and County residents and covers an area of approximately 500 square miles, and the last time the district had a rate increase approved by voters was in 1988. Complicating the problem is the number of municipalities in the County that have their own sewage systems within many of the same watersheds. It's a real mess.

Primarily because of the continuing financial problems, both St.

127

Louis City Mayor Freeman Bosley, Jr., and County Executive George Westfall asked Confluence St. Louis, a private group, to come up with suggestions. In March of this year (1995), Confluence issued a preliminary report which was followed up with public hearings.

Confluence is suggesting that a nonprofit corporation be set up that would lease MSD's operations. The corporation would be empowered to establish fees and issue revenue bonds, thus eliminating the need for voter approval. The public, however, would continue have control over the system through the MSD board, who would still be appointed by the mayor and county executive. These appointments would also require the approval of the St. Louis City Board of Aldermen and the County Council. Just this last week Confluence changed its position and said that instead of going through the County Council and Board of Aldermen, rate increases should be approved by the Public Utilities Commission. Whatever plan might be decided on, it would most likely require amendments to MSD's charter and the state constitution.

In the long haul the biggest problem facing MSD is not financial but the question of how to rehabilitate an antiquated piecemeal system in order to provide long-term adequate sanitary and stormwater system for all its customers. As I see it, in order to achieve that goal we must:

- view each individual sewer system and watershed as but a piece of the puzzle.
- incorporate all these watersheds into a single regional plan.
- develop a long-term stormwater and sanitary sewer system that will serve the entire city and county.

Ideally such a plan would either incorporate all existing systems into a single entity or into regional or watershed districts.

Now here's the tough part — if such a system is going to be expected to provide new development with adequate service while at the same time continuing to provide quality service to its existing customers, it is the sewer system district and not the individual political subdivisions which must determine if a new development meets established stormwater and sanitary standards. As I have tried to point out in this work, most of our present problems concerning urban sprawl and infrastructure breakdown are due to lack of planning or, as is more often the case, either ignoring long-term plans or setting aside established rules to accommodate special interest groups. In such cases greed usually wins out over need and reason.

I need not point out that coming up with such a workable system won't be easy. But then neither was eliminating smog in St. Louis in 1939, the creation of MSD in 1954, and the recent Wildwood incorporation. Missouri is not only the Show-Me State, but at times, especially in matters concerning the environment, has been the We'll Show-Ya state — that is, when the people get fed up and take control. The most noticeable example is the creation of the Missouri Conservation Commission in 1936, the 1/8% cent sales tax for conservation in 1976, and the 1984 1/10% cent tax for parks and soil conservation. All three of these were achieved through the initiative petition process.

One thing for sure, if the job is going to be done right, like the above examples, it will have to be done by the citizens and outside the political arena. It's time we learned our lesson — no more County tree ordinance committee and stormwater hearing charades.

WELDON SPRING

In late August I met with Stephen McCracken, Project Manager at the Weldon Spring Site Remedial Action Project. My purpose was to fill in some blanks in my research and check on the the present status of the project. Gaining access to the site felt like entering a military post during war time. But that was only at the entrance — once inside the office there was a very friendly atmosphere. Mr. McCracken greeted me with a smile and handshake, invited me into his office, offered me a seat and pulled one up next to me. None of this behind-the-big-wide-table stuff. For a second I thought, is this the project manager or public relations director? It didn't take me long, however, to realize he was for real.

As we reviewed the history of the site, he paused and gave a brief summary. "This was hard on the local residents. The government came in and took over the area. The people that worked here thought that they had a job for life, and then the whole operation was shut down and they were left with this mess. There was a lot of anger over the whole thing." At another point in the discussion about the operation of the facility he paused and said, "You know, we shouldn't judge the past by today's values." The projected completion of the cleanup is 2002. As for the large storage cell that will encase the solid waste, a few design features still need to be determined.

Following our discussion, Mr. McCracken called in Lisa Callwell to give me a tour of the site. It was a mind-boggling experience. All the buildings had been razed and the material had been sorted and stored according to its composition. Liquid contaminants were stored in barrels and placed in the one remaining building. Lined retention ponds were closely monitored as was the air quality.

Contaminated waters from the ponds and quarry pose the greatest health risks. While the St. Charles County wellfield that supplies approximately 60,000 local residents to date is safe to drink, contamination is moving in that direction.

It was easy to see why the projected cost of the cleanup is close to $1 billion. That the majority of the waste is low-level radiation seems to suggest overkill — but then I think about the Francis Howell High School, the August A. Busch and Weldon Spring Wildlife Areas that borders the property, and the St. Charles wellfield beneath. One thing I did feel good about was the positive attitude of everyone I came in contact with. They seem proud of their work and I believe that if it's humanly possible to get the job done right, these are the folks who can do it. God willin' and the Superfund don't run dry!

WILDWOOD

At 11:30 a.m. on September 1, the long-delayed incorporation of Wildwood became official: on that day it became the 91st municipality in St. Louis County. Over 300 people attended the incorporation ceremony at Babler State Park. Following the ceremony the city's first official meeting was held. The new interim government is made up of a 16-member council, a mayor, treasurer, marshal and police judge which under state law were appointed by the St. Louis County government. In a spirit of cooperation the County Council was presented with a list of 8 pro and 8 anti-incorporation candidates that the two groups had agreed upon.

Earlier on June 15, the County Council had approved all but two of the individuals on the list. Jerry Corcoran, Democratic Councilman from St. Ann, insisted that the council appoint at least two pro-development members. Later the Wildwood Council choose David Glaser, Associate Superintendent of the Francis Howell School District, who was neutral on the Wildwood issue, as their Mayor.

Also on the above date, St. Louis County Executive George Westfall also announced that he was dropping the County's court challenge of the February election when voters approved Wildwood incorporation. Westfall was taking the above action because the state had recently passed, and Governor Carnahan had signed, a new law resurrecting the old Boundary Commission that the Missouri Supreme Court had ruled unconstitutional. The new Commission, like the old one, will have the final say on whether issues pertaining to incorporation, annexation and consolidation should be placed on the ballot.

Shortly after their meeting, Mayor Glaser informed County Counselor John Ross that the new city would take whatever action would be necessary to overturn the County's assignment of 39 miles of arterial roads to Wildwood without transferring the money needed to maintain them. Glaser pointed out that this was the first time that the County Council had transferred roads to a municipality without transferring such funds. Other than this particular issue, which Wildwood proponents claim was a punitive action on the part of the County, Wildwood seems to be off and running.

In another matter related to incorporation, on November 7, South County residents will vote on the incorporation of South Pointe, a 47.7-

square mile parcel of land extending south of the city limits to the Jefferson County line and west to Tesson Ferry Road (highway 21). If approved, it will become the County's second largest city in land area next to Wildwood. With nearly 105,000 residents, it will also become the largest in population. Unlike the Wildwood proponents, the main concern is not development — that's a done deal — but the fear of being annexed to death in bits and pieces by neighboring municipalities. The annexation, if approved, would take in all but the very upper headwaters of the Gravois Creek.

Also, if approved, the County's remaining unincorporated area will be down to about half of its original size. Recently, the League of Women Voters has been advocating that the remaining unincorporated areas in the County be annexed by neighboring cities or forced to incorporate.

FEDERAL AND STATE LEGISLATION

An enduring political stereotype in this country has been that the Republicans represent the rich and big business and the Democrats the working man. I've always had something of a problem with that generalization. I personally believe, like Jefferson, that the government that governs least governs best, and that if the economy is doing poorly there will be little time and money spent on environmental concerns. In the past many of the Republican programs that have been viewed as totally pro-business I feel also benefit the "working class." Yeah, I know that's the trickle-down theory, but it really does work that way. For sure, workers don't receive paychecks and wage increases if companies don't make a profit or if they go belly-up.

On the other hand, if workers don't receive their fair share of the economic pie, they won't be able to increase consumer demand which "keeps the smokestacks toiling." Then too if the government expects welfare recipients to go to work and become self-sufficient they need to be realistic about what's a livable minimum wage.

When asked my political philosophy my response is that I believe in basic Republican economics and Democratic environmentalism. Strange bedfellows! In the past few decades, as our County continued to grow in environmental consciousness, I tended to vote for sound economic policy.

But, that was then and this is now. As my Grampa Taylor use to say "the proof's in the pudding" and "you got to call a spade a spade." So, using that guideline and looking at what the Republican-controlled Congress has been cooking up and trying to dole out to the environment — what can I say? If sound economic policy means that progress and pollution are a given — "that you can't have one without the other"— count me out!

In short, I believe if the present Republican environmental agenda is passed we will have undone most of the environmental progress achieved since the first Earth Day celebration and the birth of the EPA twenty-five years ago. I wish it was otherwise but the facts seem to speak for themselves.

There are two approaches to weakening present environmental laws and policies. One is to limit the authority of regulatory agencies and/or drastically reduce funding. The other is to return such powers to the states. Of course, a basic flaw with the latter is that even if individual states choose to establish tough air and water standards they have no power to regulate neighboring polluters.

Congress's number one target has been the EPA. At this time it looks as if its funding for the next fiscal year will be cut by 30 percent, and that an additional plan is to drastically limit or eliminate EPA regulations protecting the public's health and the environment.

Legislation has also been advanced to restrict the ability of the EPA to enforce the "right-to-know" law that now requires around 23,000 manufacturing facilities to issue annual reports on emissions of 651 chemicals listed by the agency. In addition, current proposals would not allow new chemicals and industries to be added to the list. Also there is a plan to "delist" (remove) thousands of Superfund sites.

Representative Tom DeLay, Republican from Texas, summed up the attitude shared by a number of his colleagues when he said on the House floor that, "the EPA, the Gestapo of government, pure and simple has been one of the major claw-hooks that the government maintains on the backs of our constituents."

The Endangered Species Act will also be revised this year, and the plan is to place a moratorium on adding new species to the list. Deep cuts are also planned for the Department of Science and other natural resource programs. Among these is a proposal to end the Interior Department's National Biological Service created in 1993 to inventory our country's plants and animals. Many legislators feared that the study would be used to add new species to the endangered species list and place additional limits on private property.

In another proposal federal agencies would have to assign dollar value to health and safety when issuing new regulations. This of course will add cost, increasing red tape and the amount of time it would take to implement new regulations. This same bill would also make it easier for businesses to block federal environmental regulations in court.

There are also a number of proposals that would make it easier for industries and ranchers to exploit public resources such as mining, grazing, forest reserves — even allowing the states and the private sector to acquire or manage large chunks of federal property.

Last but not least there are many other anti-environmental proposals masked under such catchy headings as "private property rights" and "unfunded mandates." Some even have a degree of merit, but most have an underlying purpose of eliminating or greatly reducing the Federal Government's ability to protect the public health and the environment. At present none of these proposals has been passed by both houses and signed by the President into law.

Here in Missouri a similar attitude exists. The most blatant example was a bill that, had it not been defeated, would have prohibited government agencies from releasing information about polluters if the company on its own informed the government about it.

In a similar matter, the general assembly removed $22 million from the state budget that had been earmarked for setting up a tougher auto emissions program for the St. Louis area, and then in an act of defiance set aside $1 for the program. Whenever an area has a "moderate" problem, the EPA asks the state to take some tangible action to reduce pollution. The new inspection stations was one possible choice; so would have been the use of reformulated fuel that would help reduce ozone levels which is what the DNR had suggested. But when station owners complained to the state legislator that it would increase gas prices, the state asked stations to switch to fuels that have a lower rate of evaporation and is a bit cheaper than reformulated fuel. This is what was finally decided upon but it is considered the least effective of the three and ozone levels continue to increase.

Because the area's ozone levels have been increasing over the last several years, the EPA has classified our air quality as a "moderate" problem, and because this year we have set a record for exceeding these standards the EPA could reclassify our air-quality as serious, which could lead to EPA sanctions. In anticipation of government action, last year the legislature ordered the state attorney general to file a suit in federal court against the authority of Congress and EPA to impose sanctions.

Two factors seem to have been overlooked here. One is that the American Lung Association has pointed out that EPA ozone safety levels are actually too low, and second a recent study of six metropolitan areas, including St. Louis, showed a direct correlation between air pollution and increases in mortality rates.

As for positive state legislation, the general assembly this spring passed a billboard law. Missouri ranks third among states in the total number billboards — 28,000 — and is the only state that doesn't allow local communities to pass ordinances stricter than state law. The new law allows the State Highway Commission to designate roads as scenic byways and to ban new billboards. The law does not affect existing billboards, but it's a beginning.

On the lighter side, the legislature did vote the mule the official state animal and designated the square dance as the state folk dance.

14 - New Business

Since completing the main text, some new issues have developed.

TYSON RESEARCH CENTER

Early in July, Washington University fired Tyson Research Center's director, Richard Coles, and announced that they were planning to close the 2,000-acre preserve. This announcement shocked local environmentalists, for the rumors soon spread that the university was planning to sell the property. The Tyson area is a vital link in the Meramec River greenway and at present is home to the Wild Canid Survival and Research Center as well as the temporary headquarters of the World Bird Sanctuary. It should be noted that neither of these are university facilities; both rent space at the Center.

The university issued a one-page response to inquiries as to their plans for the property. It stated that operations at Tyson would be significantly reduced for several years, during which time they would review the future use of Tyson for university purposes." During the interim the land will remain undisturbed. This move, the university claims, should save the institution around $250,000 a year.

Many individuals still fear that the land might eventually be sold to developers. Some feel that to do so would violate the spirit of the conditions under which the university acquired the property. During World War II the federal government used the Tyson tract, originally 2,373 acres, as a powder storage and ammunition testing range. In 1950 St. Louis County purchased the property for half its market value on condition that it be used for recreational purposes. With the outbreak of the Korean War in 1951, the government took the property back and it was once again used for storing ammunition. By 1962 the Federal Government was again ready to dispose of the property. The County tried to regain the property, but the bulk of it (2000 acres) was given to Washington University. The County received the remaining acreage which today makes up Lone Elk and West Tyson county parks.

In the university's application for the site it said that it would use the property to build a major research center which would be used for a large number of projects. The list included among other things environmental engineering, medicine, biology and earth science. On October 2, 1963, the United States government agreed to transfer the property to the university on condition that it be used continuously for educational purposes for twenty years. The fair market value of the property at the time was set at $1,004,000. Now that over thirty years have passed, the university is free to do whatever it wishes with the property. The problem is that some individuals and organizations claim that the university never fulfilled their obligation and thus should give up the property. True, other than conducting a few wildlife studies the university has fallen well short of its once lofty goals. The university has primarily used the property for storage and rental property, as well as a place to house dogs and other animals used by the medical school for a variety of experiments. These functions will soon be moved to other locations. The university, of course, maintains that it has met its obligations.

Since Washington University made their announcement, St. Louis County has shown interest in acquiring the site. County Executive Westfall said the County was going to explore the possibility of adding it to the county park system. County Councilman Greg Quinn strongly supports such an idea and said that acquiring the property would make it possible for the state and county to work a deal that would provide road access to the south portion of Castlewood State Park which currently is closed off by the research center. Whatever the future holds for Tyson, I feel that one way or another it will continue to remain an important link in the Meramec River greenway — the public is going to insist on it!

NEW WASTE SITE DISCOVERED

In August St. Louisans learned that the DNR had been investigating an 11-acre site in north St. Louis for some time. The property was once owned by the Great Lakes Container Corporation. In 1986 the company abandoned the site and because it owed $70,000 in back taxes, the property was taken over by the city in 1994.

Great Lakes was in the business of reconditioning 55-gallon steel drums that had contained a variety of toxins. Some were shipped from as far away as Canada. On an average work day 1,200 barrels were cleaned and reconditioned for resale. According to the former plant supervisor, Robert O'Brien, after washing out the barrels the chemical sludge was shoveled into new containers and then stacked in a ravine on the property. According to an August 8 Post-Dispatch article, O'Brien claims that in November of 1984 the company buried over 500 of these barrels on site to avoid paying several hundred dollars per barrel to have them disposed of properly at a hazardous waste facility. Both DNR and EPA are concerned that the waste will eventually contaminate ground water and the Mississippi which flows nearby.

This is not the first time Great Lakes has been accused of such activities. In 1980 tens of thousands of barrels of toxic waste were discovered at one of its facilities in Kingston, New Hampshire. That discovery eventu-

135

ally led to the first Superfund court case and cleanup. Because the Missouri DNR feels that the St. Louis cleanup is beyond its scope, it plans to ask the EPA to take it over as a Superfund site. Considering what's going on in Washington these days — good luck!

BROWNFIELDS

Not all the news about abandoned property has been negative. In July St. Louis was one of 15 communities to receive a $200,000 "brownfield" grant from the EPA. Brownfields are abandoned city industrial property that may have pollution problems. Most of these properties, like the Great Lakes Container Corporation site, became city property due to failure to pay back taxes. At present the city owns about 2,000 parcels which amounts to over 40 million square feet. Because of the high cost of cleaning up these areas and the pollution liability new owners can inherit when they purchase them, the prospects of these properties being rehabilitated have been extremely low.

In the past, even though a site was to be used for industrial purposes, the EPA generally required it to be cleaned to residential standards. Recently the EPA and state governments have been taking a new look at the problem and have come up with some creative ways to get these properties back into production. The $200,000 EPA grant will be used to help clean up the Martin Luther King Business Park, a 26-acre site bounded by Delmar Boulevard, Jefferson Avenue, Carr and 20th street. Under the new program the EPA will allow the area to be cleaned up to industrial standards. The Missouri DNR will oversee the cleanup. In addition the new owners will be protected from suits filed over pre-existing pollution.

Among other things, the grant will help pay for the cost of inventorying environmental problems in the business park, pay administrative expenses of a citizens advisory committee and a committee of experts who would work with businesses interested in moving into the area, and consider ways to set up a redemption fund to help businesses pay for cleanup costs that exceed initial estimates. It is hoped that this program will serve as a model for restoring other sites.

In addition to the federal government's involvement, the state recently enacted the Abandoned Property Reuse Act. A key feature of the new law allows a tax credit applied to a business's cleanup costs. While some environmentalists are skeptical about this new program, particularly the lowering of cleanup standards, to me, it seems like a move in the right direction.

CHEMICAL WARFARE TRAINING SCHOOL MOVES
TO FORT LEONARD WOOD

In late June the Defense Base Closure and Realignment Commission made its final decision to close Fort McClellan in Alabama and the move the army's chemical warfare training school and military police school to Fort Leonard Wood. While most Missourians seemed pleased by the military police move, that was not necessarily the case with the chemical warfare school. The Missouri Coalition for the Environment was particularly concerned about the haste in which the Missouri DNR approved all the needed permits required to make the move.

DNR Director David Shorr admitted that the permit approval process was on the "fast track." Shorr maintained that the DNR has been studying McClellan's operations since 1993. He was quoted by the Post as saying, "People should give us a little credit that we are smart enough to know what's coming at us." Personally, I'll give him and the DNR the benefit of the doubt on this one, but what upset me is an incident that occurred on June 7.

On June 6, Senator Howell Heflin, Democrat from Alabama, pushed through an amendment to the Senate's anti-terrorism bill which, if it hadn't been repealed the following day, might have prevented the chemical warfare school from being moved to Missouri. What his amendment did was to add the nerve gases "sarin" and "VX" to a list of hazardous materials covered by the federal Solid Waste Disposal Act. Heflin's amendment had a grandfather clause that would have exempted Department of Defense facilities in existence on the date the bill is enacted. In other words, this would allow the Army to keep the chemical school at Fort McClellan without obtaining the required environmental permits and conducting environmental impact studies which could take years. However, to move the school to Fort Leonard Wood would require such permits and studies.

It wasn't until the following day the real intent of the bill finally sunk in and the Senate repealed the amendment. But the individual who seemed the most upset about Heflin's ploy was none other than David Shorr. He was quoted by the News Services as saying, "If this is such a hazardous waste, then we will do our damnedest to see that similar stringent requirements are met at Fort McClellan."

My point is simple —why in the world is the Missouri Director of DNR lobbying to bring nerve gases and an incinerator to Missouri? I thought his job description was to protect our state's environment and enforce existing environmental rules — not work to circumvent them. One can understand the Governor and other state departments working hard to get the Army's facilities moved here. But then we must realize that the Director of the Department of Natural Resources, unlike the head of the Missouri Department of Conservation, is appointed by the Governor.

Applications for these permits were filed on March 1, 1995, and by mid-April the DNR had approved them. On April 27, the Coalition, along with several families living in the Fort Leonard Wood area, filed appeals with the Missouri Air Conservation Commission. One appeal would overturn a construction permit that would allow the Army to build an incinerator to burn hazardous waste. The Coalition maintained that the permit was issued without a public hearing and was replete with errors. They also sought a hearing to oppose DNR's request for a waiver from the state's opacity rules for the Army's fog training exercises. The waiver will allow the Army to use oil-burning generators that produce smokescreens during training exercises.

My concern is that while the move will help stimulate the local economy, which is good, will all the environmental safeguards be in place as David Shorr maintains? Sorry, but some things just don't travel very well on the "fast track."

An interesting footnote — according to a May 22 *Time* magazine article the Army plans to abandon some 2,500 tons of toxic waste in Alabama, requiring a $100 million incinerator to destroy these wastes. So, for Alabama residents, it's "good-by Fort McClellan, hello Times Beach."

15 - Promised Land

Following their prey, the First Americans discovered the Promised Land on the other side of the land bridge connecting the two continents of Asia and America — two different worlds. For millenniums this new world was a vastly rich hunting ground.

The Europeans stumbled upon it on their way to the Orient. They first cursed it for getting in the way of The Quest.

After finally having seen the forest through the trees, this land became a refuge, a safety valve from European poverty, overpopulation, broken hearts and spent dreams. It was a land vibrant, rich in resources, that spawned new dreams, hopes, promises and seemingly unlimited horizons. It was a good place to plant and build anew be fruitful and multiply. And they did.

The immigrants, their children, and their children's children took from the land — fueling economic growth, development and their unquenchable thirst for wealth. Each generation pursued their dreams and moved towards new horizons. Theirs was an unabated faith in the belief that they were indeed the chosen people; that there would always be land and resources aplenty; that our governmental, industrial and economic institutions were just the ticket. To question any of the above, to think otherwise, was downright un-American and sacrilegious.

Throughout this great adventure there were those who warned us that attainable dreams must be rooted in reality and reminded us that all the wealth we have accumulated or ever will accumulate comes from Mother Nature's bank account — and that we were using up the reserves and digging deeper and deeper into the principal.

There were times along the way that we paused and heeded some of those warnings. Particularly in this last quarter century, we seemed to have matured enough to re-examine The Quest —especially when we realized that the by-products of uncontrolled progress could be injurious to our own health.

More recently, in light of current social and economic problems, we have become increasingly aware that the very fiber of our society is being threatened. Americans have become bewildered and scared. And, as is often the case at such times, the new quest seems to be to go back to "them good old days."

Some insist that the problem is simply a family values matter, and that the only way to get out of this mess is to get right with God and teach that old-time religion. Others look for a revival in political and economic reform: if we would only revert back to when the people were more self-reliant and the government stayed out of social issues, return the power to the states, and let the business community run the economy on their terms, then every thing would be just hunky-dory.

But the fact is that we are no longer an agrarian society of 3 million souls as was the case when President Washington took office and the first Congress met. Let's face it, today we are a technologically complex society with all the blessings and curses that go with it. In 1890 the U. S. government reported that there was no longer an American frontier, and by the mid-twentieth century over a majority of our people were living in urban areas. Today it's around 90 percent.

Human society changes, whether we like it or not, whenever we change the nature of things. And the major change in our society, as I see it, is that very few of us, if any, today meet our needs, directly through the family and from the land. When one becomes dependent on others for basic needs, there is a loss of freedom and self-reliance, and it increases with each middleman that stands between us and those needs. That's just as true of modern-day farmers who practice mono-agriculture, receive farm subsidies, use chemical fertilizers and pesticides to raise their crops and gasoline and oil to plant them and get them to market on government-built roads.

One of the reasons my mother's family was little affected by the Great Depression was that they owned their own home and land and didn't put all their eggs in one basket. Not only did they grow all their own food, they worked the land with mules and horses and recycled their waste back onto the fields.

Like the people, as a country becomes less resource self-sufficient, it becomes less free to steer its own course and avoid being manipulated by world events. Back about the time I was born, our country was producing over 90 percent of its oil needs — and now we're importing around 50 percent. This in spite of two OPEC wake-up calls. True, we made a feeble attempt at developing alternative energy and once again becoming energy self-sufficient, but it didn't take long for the old greed factor to kick in. For one, we resented the government mandating cleaner-burning and more fuel-efficient cars, and two, the embargos were eventually dropped and so did the price of foreign oil.

It's my opinion that our number one national defense strategy should be to become resource self-sufficient. Sure, we need a strong military to protect our freedoms from foreign aggression, but the fact that our county got involved in Middle Eastern politics decades ago because we coveted their vast oil reserves is a major reason we ended up having to draw a line in the sand.

In the latter parts of this work I have tried to lay out many of our current state and local environmental problems. Most are typical of the

140

concerns experienced throughout the country. Then, too, like all things in nature, these problems extend well beyond what we usually refer to as "the environment."

A major problem is that while our present economic system is extremely efficient in meeting our material wants, needs and greed, it ignores many of our basic personal, family and community needs. It particularly short-circuits many of the genetically programmed developmental needs of our children. Many children today miss out altogether or have deferred important transitions, vision quests, and rites of passage. Thus, more and more of us are less prepared for adult relationships and responsibility.

Education institutions outside the "traditional community" settings can only do so much. The problem is that many of our basic developmental needs can't be met through artificial means. They need real life, not artificially programmed life experiences, at the right place, the right time, and some — with just the right folks. Human society can't continue to deny our biological and cultural heritage.

The problem is that even when corrective measures are obvious, logical, and rational, if they threaten our present philosophies, behavior, and particularly our economic structure, they are quickly labeled radical and unrealistic.

It's important for us to have a place that we belong to and it to us — especially for children during those developmental years. It's sad that today not only the land but our communities are viewed as commodities. Thus, most of our "belongings" have become things as opposed to ideas and values, people and places.

If it's true that "the proof is in the pudding" and "you got to call a spade a spade," it seems clear by our collective actions, or our lack of action, that the majority of us value things and the monetary value of things over our professed "traditional values." "Talk is cheap." There are exceptions, of course, and that's why I feel especially good and hopeful about the Wildwood experience. Here we have another historic example of citizens willing to put their time and money where their values are.

While most of us want the government off our backs, the truth of the matter is that the more we lose our sense of place, family ties and sense of community, the more we have relegated our family, clan, tribal and community responsibilities to institutions and governments. And, no matter how hard they try, they make darn poor substitutes.

So, how did it happen? Of course, it's all very complex, but basically I think that with the loss and weakening of the above basics we also began to lose control. With the loss of "belonging" goes the loss of unity and direction. When humankind had no choice but to work together and adapt to the laws of nature or perish, our course and direction were a lot clearer.

With the dawning of the industrial revolution we began to enter the fast track, and progress was the battle cry that felled the trees and laid the tracks to new and often false horizons. The problem was we didn't know where we where going. There was no plan, no vote — just lots of blind faith. But for the majority of us that was OK because progress is good! "Progress is our most important product." "You can't stop progress." "Consume, consume, consume, develop, invest."

Blind faith is one of those petrified opinions Mark Twain wrote about. Twain also defined faith as "believin' in what you know ain't true." Ouch! I see it a little different than Twain, which I know is close to arguing with God. But I personally believe that people tend to have faith in those things they have no control over, and those things they have no control over, they have faith are good. You know, " When your number's up, your number's up," which is always popular during periods of war. Then there's "Everything that happens has a purpose" and "everything works out for the best." And for the really tough ones, "God works in mysterious ways." Ever since we moved beyond adapting and began manipulating nature, we have felt the need to be in control.

My purpose here is not to make light of people's beliefs, but to point out that some generalizations are no longer true — and some never were.

As I wrote this section I thought back to what Stephen McCracken, the project manager of the Weldon Spring cleanup site, said: "We can't judge the past by today's values." I buy that. But it's also time to realize that we can't base today's actions and set goals in accordance with the way things used to be!

The current Congressional view is that we must accept human habitat degradation as an economic given. So instead of banning toxic pollutants, the government will now be assessing what is the maximum level we can tolerate. And, again, we will be placing a dollar value on what it costs to protect the people's health. It's interesting that we DARE our children to be drug-and-chemical free when at the same time our society has embraced chemical dependency. The agriculture industry insists, and at this point they are probably right, that in order to feed the masses we have no choice but to use chemical fertilizers and pesticides. However, if we had kept our human population within a naturally sustainable balance and depended less on mono-agriculture, then that might not be necessary. It's a shame when we let things get to the point where all our choices are bad ones.

To complicate matters even more, now we have the information superhighway — the Internet, which like other forms of technology is a mixed blessing. Like industry and the mass media, it will exert a tremendous force upon our society, and like the other two, we are already finding out that it will be difficult if not downright impossible to control its negative forces. So now we've gone from wilderness to Internet, and where do we go from here? The scary part is that nobody knows, and no one's in control!

I only know that if we want our children to fly like eagles and see truth, love, and life more clearly than in past generations, they're gonna need pure water, clear blue skies, lots of sunshine —a healthy habitat here on earth — and a few brier patches scattered here and there sure wouldn't hurt.

It seems logical, rational, and inevitable to me that if we keep messing up, soon we will have lost all our "belongings." And where can the children go from here— from this, their promised land?

* * *

HIGHWAY LIFE

Seein' love and life in living color
Hearin' truths in stereo.
That super information highway taking us —
To where? Nobody knows!

Grab a brass ring, slide into the loop
We're all on a fast track.
We don't know were we're goin' man,
And, uh, oh — we can't go back.

Things aren't like they used to be
Back in what we called
"Them good old days."
They were black and white and mono
Not like our TVs and stereos today.

The Government always told their truths
Represented the best of us.
Made us feel real comfortable
In our deepest prej-u-dice.

Love and life in living color, truths in stereo
Surfin' on the highway can get scary
Learning things
We didn't want to know.

"Loyalty to petrified opinion
Never broke a chain or freed a human soul."
Sincerely yours, Mark Twain
He said many years ago.

Seein' love and life in living color
Hearin' truths in stereo.
That information superhighway taking us —
To where? Nobody knows!

Grab a brass ring, slide into the loop
We're all on a fast track.
We don't know were we're goin' man,
And, uh, oh — we can't go back.

* * *

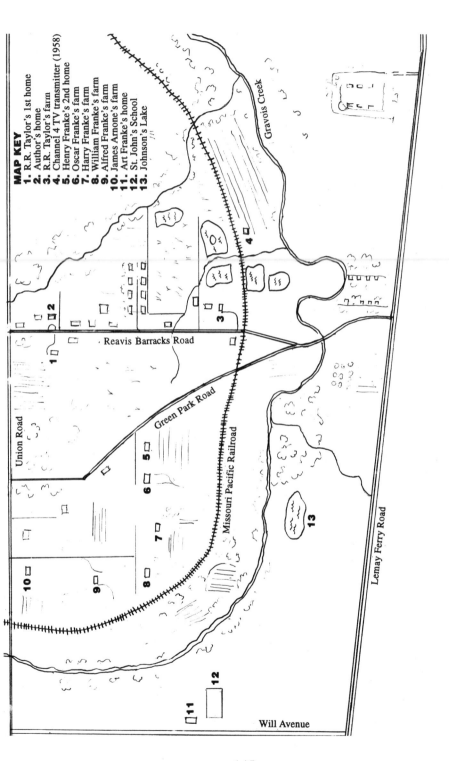

Gravois Creek Map, circa 1957.

145

Gravois Creek area, 1960 — aerial photo by permission from SURDEX Corporation.

Gravois Creek area, 1994 — aerial photo by permission from SURDEX Corporation.

TIMELINE

PART I: WILDERNESS TO STATEHOOD

900 - 1300 A. D.
Mississippian culture centered at Cahokia reaches its peak and then disappears.

1500's
1541 -...............De Soto, the Spanish explorer, first recorded European to see the Mississippi River.

1600's
1607 -...............Jamestown founded by the English.
1608 -...............Quebec founded by the French.
1673 - June 17..Father Marquette and Louis Joliet reach the Mississippi at the mouth of the Wisconsin River.
1682 - April 9 ..La Salle reaches the mouth of the Mississippi and claims the watershed for France.
1699 -...............Cahokia founded by Society of Foreign Missions. First Euro-American settlement in St. Louis area.

1700's
1700 - ....Mission of the Immaculate Conception re-established at the mouth of the River Des Peres. First Euro-American settlement in Missouri.
1750 -...............Ste. Genevieve founded.
1762 - Nov.13..France, by secret treaty of Fontainebleau cedes territory west of Mississippi to Spain.Word of treaty doesn't reach area for two years.
1763 - Dec. .....Treaty of Paris ends French and Indian War and grants England French lands east of the Mississippi.
Laclede selects St. Louis as site for his fur-trading post.
1767 -...............Carondelet founded by Clement Delor de Treget.
1768 -...............St. Charles founded by Louis Blanchette.
1775 -...............Start of American Revolution.
1780 - May 26 .Battle of St. Louis: Emanuel Hess and Jean Marie Ducharme, along with large group of Indians attack St. Louis and Cahokia. Attack fails.
1783 - Sept. 3...Treaty of Paris ends American Revolution.
The new country extends west to the Mississippi and north to Canada.
1785 -...............Florissant founded.
First cardboard box manufactured in Philadelphia.
1793 -...............Cape Girardeau founded by Louis Lorimier.
1794 -...............Marais de Liards (Bridgeton) is founded.
1796 -...............Spain opens Louisiana to Americans.
1798 -...............First Spanish census shows St. Louis has population of 925.
Daniel Boone moves to Missouri.

1800's
1800 - Oct. 1....Treaty of San Ildefonso returns Louisiana territory to France.
1803 -...............St. Louis has population of 1,000.
April 30.Louisiana Purchase Treaty.
1804 - March 1 Upper Louisiana transferred to the Americans at St. Louis.

148

1805 - March 3.Territory of Louisiana established; St. Louis becomes seat of
           government.
1810 -...............Peter Durand of England patents the tin can.
1812 - June 4 ...Territory of Louisiana becomes Territory of Missouri.
           Oct. 1 ....First General Assembly of the Territory meets.
1816 -...............Missouri Territory becomes third-class territory.
1817 -...............First petition for statehood circulated.
           Territory has 60,000 residents.
1818 -...............Missouri Territory petitions Congress to become a state.
           First steamboat ("Zebulon M. Pike") reaches St. Louis.
1820 - March 6 Missouri Enabling Act passed and approved by President Monroe.
           State Constitutional Convention held.
           Aug. 10 First state election held.
1821 - Aug. 28 Missouri becomes 24th state.
           St. Charles, Manchester, and Gravois roads declared first state roads.

PART II : ROOTED

1830 -...............St. Louis population is 6,694.
1840 -...............St. Louis population 16,649.
1842 -...............Henry Kayser plans first St. Louis sewage system — dumps sewage
           into caves and sinkholes.
1845 -...............Mehlville founded by Charles Mehl.
1848 -...............Large number of Germans come to Missouri — called the"forty-
           eighters."
1849 -...............Cholera epidemic in St. Louis kills about 10 percent of city's
           population.
1850 -...............St. Louis population is 77,860.
1851 -...............Samuel Curtis builds first trunk sewer system in St. Louis — sewage
           now dumped into the Mississippi.
           Missouri Plank Road Law passed — plank toll roads were to be built
           on all heavily traveled routes.
1852 -...............The Cumberland Road now extends to St. Louis (Highway 40).
           First rail service—Pacific R. R. completes section between St. Louis
           and Kirkwood.
1855 -...............Iron Mountain Railroad built to mining area in southern Missouri.
1858 -...............Overland stage makes runs between St. Louis and California.
1859 -...............Horse-drawn passenger cars first used in St. Louis.

1860's

1861 -...............Start of American Civil War: Governor Claiborne F. Jackson tries to
           take state out of Union but fails.
1865 -...............Civil War ends.
1869 -...............First railroad bridge is built over Missouri River at St. Charles.
           First transcontinental railroad completed.
           Plastic industry begins when John Hyatt of America creates first man-
           made celluloid.

1870's

1870 -...............St. Louis population is 320,000.
1872 -...............Congress establishes Yellowstone National Park.
1874 -...............Eads Bridge is opened.
1875 -...............New state constitution allows St. Louis County to establish home rule.
           St. Louis elects board of freeholders to design plan for separation.
1876 -...............St. Louis Forest Park is acquired.
           St. Louis City and County split approved.
           St. Louis City left with 61.8 square miles, St. Louis County 497 square
           miles.
1877 -...............St. Louis County population is 31,888. New County government
           begins.

1880's
1884 -...............Electric power service comes to St. Louis.
1886 -...............Cable cars begin operating in St. Louis.
................George Bird Grinnell founds first Audubon Society.
1889 -...............Bill passed to establish national forest lands.
1890 -...............St. Louis City population at 575,000.
................Development reaches city limits then spreads into St. Louis County.
................Electric trolleys begin service in St. Louis.
1892 -...............Sierra Club founded.
................The bottle cap invented.
1895 -...............Gillete invents disposable razor blade.
1900's
1900 -...............Method for clarifying water in St. Louis is perfected.
1904 -...............St. Louis World's Fair. River Des Peres where it runs through Forest Park is temporarily boarded over to hide sewage.
................U. S. Postal Service authorizes permit mailing — beginning of junk mail industry.
1908 -...............First paper cup appears on the market.
1812 -...............Cellophane introduced.
1913 -...............St. Louis Zoo is opened.
1914 -...............Gravois becomes first concrete road to be built in area.
1916 -...............County passes $3 million dollar bond issue to construct concrete roads.
................National Park Service established.
1917 -...............U. S. Enters World War I.
1918 -...............World War I ends.
1923 -...............Hawthorn named Missouri state flower.
1924 -...............All Indians made U. S. Citizens.
................Smoke Regulation Commission created to license and inspect new coal furnaces in the city of St. Louis.
1926 -...............The Planning Federation, a regional planning commission, is formed.
1927 -...............Bluebird named official Missouri state bird.
................"Black Christmas" of 1927 due to smog in St. Louis.
1928 -...............St. Louis County Planning Association formed. First regional planning organization whose main goal was to get state to allow establishment of an official Planning Commission.
1929 -...............Beginning of Great Depression.
................Depression will create many area public work projects.
1930's
1930 -...............St. Louis County population 211,593. Half of county residents still engaged in rural occupations.
1935 -...............Regional Planning Commission formed.
................Canned beer introduced.
1936 -...............National Wildlife Federation founded.
................Missouri Conservation Commission established by voters.
1939 -..............."Black Tuesday" — worst smog ever recorded in St. Louis.
................First no deposit, no-return bottled beer introduced.
1940's
1940 - April ....St. Louis Board of Aldermen passes bill banning Illinois soft coal.
1941 -...............American enters World War II.
................State passes County Planning Enabling Act allowing Class 1 counties to appoint a County Planning Commission with power to establish zoning, subdivision control, and building setback laws in unincorporated areas of the county.
1942 - April ....Mallinckrodt Chemical Works agrees to purify uranium for atomic bomb.
1943 -...............Ball-point pen and aerosol can invented.
1944 -...............Dow Chemical creates styrofoam.

150

1945 - Aug. 7 ..Atomic bomb dropped on Hiroshima.
New state constitution provides for charter government by counties over 85,000.
1946 -...............First St. Louis County Zoning Ordinance adopted dealing with subdivision developments.
All of the county north and west of Lindbergh was zoned one-acre lots.
1949 -..............."Missouri Waltz" named official state song.
Charter Commission of St. Louis County drafts charter proposal for voter approval.

1950's
1950 -...............St. Louis County population is 406,349.
1951 -...............The Nature Conservancy founded.
New St. Louis County Government Charter approved.
Jefferson Barracks Historical Park and Sylvan Springs Park acquired.
St. Louis Urban Expressway Report issued. It suggests building three major expressways — Mark Twain, Daniel Boone and Ozark.
St. Louis County Planning Commission proposes master plan for parks.
1952 -...............Major industrial growth in county leads Planning Commission to propose agricultural zoning to preserve open space.
1953 -...............State Park Board created.
1954 -...............Acid-resistant can lining developed for soft drinks.
1954 -...............Metropolitan St. Louis Sewer District approved by voters.
1955 -...............Clean Air Act passed.
County Charter creates Department of Planning.
1956 -...............Mallinckrodt builds first commercial uranium-fuel production plant at Hematite, Missouri.
World's first photovoltaic power plant (solar energy) developed by Bell Laboratories.
Federal government provides federal funds for construction of sewage treatment plants.
1957 -...............Mallinckrodt's Weldon Spring plant in St. Charles County goes into production.

PART III: BEYOND THE BRIER PATCH

1960's
1960 -...............Populations of St. Louis City 750,026; County 703,532.
Department of Planning publishes General Land Use Plan.
1962 -...............*Silent Spring* by R. Carson is published.
1963 -...............Bi-State Transit begins operation.
St. Louis Regional Industrial Development Corporation (RID) established.
1964 -...............Ozark National Scenic Riverways created.
Wilderness Act Passed.
1965 -...............Federal Clean Air and Water Quality Act passed.
New County Zoning Ordinance based on 1960 Land Use Plan is adopted.
East-West Gateway Coordinating Council begins operations.
April 8 ..County passes new zoning ordinance which allowed developers to mix single and multiple family and townhouse on same site. Also allowed 6,000 square foot family residence.
Department of planning published "The Challenge of Growth, A Study of Major County And Regional Park Needs," calling for the expansion of county parks.
1966 -...............Weldon Spring plant shut down.
1967 -...............First time County begins to allow industrial use in areas that had been zoned rural.

1967 -...............$25 million park bond issue fails in the County by 376 votes.
1968 -...............Army makes crude cleanup of Weldon Spring.
Nation Wild and Scenic Rivers Act and National Trails Act passed.
New County Charter adopted. It provided that recommendations of Planning Commission could only be overruled by two-thirds vote of County Council members.
1969 -...............Northeastern Pharmaceutical & Chemical Company began producing dioxin as a byproduct at Verona, Missouri.
National Environmental Policy Act passed (NEPA).

1970's
1970 -...............Population of St. Louis City 622,236; St. Louis County 951,671.
April 22 First Earth Day celebration.
Environmental Protection Agency established (EPA).
Workers bring suit against National Lead Plant (St. Louis). Plant eventually closed.
1971 -...............Russell Bliss begins spraying dioxin at 27 Eastern Missouri sites.
Greenpeace established.
1972 -...............Federal Water Pollution Control Act passed to "restore and maintain the physical, chemical and biological integrity of the nation's waters."
Use of DDT banned in the United States.
1973 -...............Congress passes Endangered Species Act.
Last nuclear plant approved in U. S.
First OPEC oil embargo.
1974 -...............Missouri Department of Natural Resources established.
Danger to ozone from CFC's reported.
1975 -...............Hole in the ozone over Antarctica first observed.
1976 -...............Missouri 1/8 % cent sales tax for conservation passed by voters.
1977 -...............Missouri Hazardous Waste Act passed.
St. Louis County Parks Bond Issue passed by voters.

PART IV: REALITY CHECK
1979 -...............World population reaches five billion.
Three Mile Island nuclear shutdown.
Second OPEC oil embargo.
Missouri Division of Energy created.

1980's
1980 -...............Federal Superfund established.
Earth First! established.
1882 - Oct. 27 .Environmental Defense Fund releases list of 14 confirmed and 41 suspected dioxin sites in Missouri.
Nuclear Waste Policy Act passed.
Dec. 23 .Federal and state government announce Times Beach evacuation.
1983 - Feb. 22 .Times Beach buy-out announced.
1984 -...............Union Electric Callaway Nuclear Plant on-line.
Missouri voters approve 1/10% sales tax for state parks and soil conservation.
Missouri State Superfund Law passed.
1985 -...............Honeybee named official state insect.
EPA claim that dioxin is most dangerous chemical known.
1986 - Sept. .....Chernobyl nuclear disaster.
Last Times Beach resident relocated.
U. S. Department of Energy begins new Weldon Spring cleanup.
1988 -...............1/10% sales tax for state parks and soil extended by voters.
Use of chlordane banned in the United States.
Sept. 29 Times Beach cleanup record of decision announced.
1989 -...............Federal government announces removal of nuclear waste in St. Louis and waste cleanup at Weldon Spring.

1990's

1990 - Nov. 6 ..Non-binding referendums on nuclear waste storage in St. Louis and Times Beach incinerator held — both receive no votes.

1991 - May 21 .Dr. Vernon Houk at Columbia, Missouri, in "Dioxin Update" states that evacuation of Times Beach was a mistake.

1992 - Dec. 18 .Wildwood supporters submit petition for incorporation to St. Louis County Boundary Commission asking that issue be placed on Nov. 1994 ballot.

1993 -...............Missouri Supreme Court rules St. Louis Metropolitan Sewer District 1992 fee increase in violation of Hancock amendment. MSD, however, does not refund money.

Jan. ....County Council sets up Tree Ordinance Committee.

Missouri Supreme Court landmark decision (Heins Implement Co. vs. Missouri Highway and Transportation Commission) adopts new "doctrine of reasonable use."

Sept. 22 Area hit by major storm, New Ballwin bridge over Kiefer Creek torn out by flood: St. Louis County said it didn't have the money to repair or replace it.

Sept. 7 ..Tree Ordinance draft submitted to County's legal department, never to be seen again.

1994 - May ......Missouri Supreme Court rules St. Louis County Boundary Commission is unconstitutional.

July 28 ..County Council votes not to place Wildwood issue on November ballot.

Sept. .....New 2,000-page dioxin report supports 1985 study and says that even low levels of dioxin can cause health risks.

Nov. 5 ..Circuit Court Judge Kenneth Romines rules that Wildwood issue should be placed on February 7 ballot. The County government and cities of Chesterfield and Ellisville appeal judge's ruling.

Federal study states incineration of dioxin at Times Beach carried minimal health risks.

Dec. 16 .David Shorr of DNR signs draft permit allowing incinerator to be built.

Dec. 29 .St. Louis County Council sets emission level from Times Beach incinerator at 0.15 nanograms.

1995 - Feb. 7 ...Wildwood incorporation approved by voters by over sixty percent.

Feb. 9 ...County Council refuses to set-up interim Wildwood government until Missouri Supreme Court rules on appeals.

Mar. 29 .Missouri Court of Appeals rules St. Louis Metropolitan Sewer District must refund $40 million in rate increases to its customers. MSD appeals decision.

April 4 ..Missourians amend Article VI Section 8 of state constitution allowing state to pass laws that apply to individual counties.

May 2 ....Dr. Morris Cranmer falsly reported to the St. Louis County Monitoring Committee that the dioxin blood levels of residents living near the Vertac dioxin incinerator had dropped during the three years it was in operation.

July 2 ....14 protesters arrested at the Times Beach dioxin incinerator site.

Aug. 15 .U. S. District Judge John F. Nangle rules against the County's air pollution ordinance regulating dioxin emissions at Times Beach incinerator.

Sept. 1 ...Wildwood becomes the 91st municipality in St. Louis County.

A portion of the profits from this book is donated to the Missouri Environmental Fund, which includes the following organizations:

Bridging the Gap
Conservation Foundation of Missouri Charitable Trust
EarthWays
Friends of the Washington University Tyson Research Center
Gateway Trailnet
Heartland All Species Project
Meramec River Recreation Association
Mississippi River Basin Alliance
Missouri Audubon Council
Missouri Coalition for the Environment Foundation
Missouri Parks Association
The Missouri Prairie Foundation
Open Space Council
Ozark Regional Land Trust
Scenic Missouri
St. Louis Audubon Society

For more information about any of the above organizations or the Missouri Environmental Fund write to:
Missouri Environmental Fund
P.O. Box 63349
St. Louis, Missouri 63163
or call 314-771-6668.

For more information about the ongoing work of Kestrel Productions, contact the author, Roger W. Taylor, at:
Kestrel Productions
674 Meramec Drive
Ballwin, Missouri 63021-7232.